FINDING YOUR SPIRITUAL DNA

THE ANGEL CODE:

Vol I. Tapping into the Secret of your Spiritual DNA, Miracle Making by the Technology of the Angel Code, God's messengers of miracles, spiritual conversations, prayers, and soul guardians.

BY SARAH NYAMUSWA

Book Art Cover by Tawana Dete

A stunning blend of adventure and mysticism, fact, science and the politics of Angels. A look into the world of Angel choirs reads like a science fiction thriller, but is in fact a decoded artifact of the sacred language, that also allows you to learn which Angels assigned to you at birth give you these same attributes to make magical shifts in our lives Revealing Your Spiritual DNA: The Angel Choirs are a deeply sacred portrayal of an alien, divine society more complete and detailed than any author in the field has managed…a story so absorbing equally for it's supra meta divine action, power and philosophical vistas.

"As I gazed on the creatures, I saw one wheel on the ground next to each of the four-faced creatures. As for the appearance and structure of the wheels, they gleamed like beryl. All four had the same form; the appearance and structure of each was as of two wheels cutting through each other. And when they moved, each could move in the direction of any of its four quarters; they did not veer when they moved. Their rims were tall and frightening, for the rims of all four were covered all over with eyes. And when the creatures moved forward, the wheels moved at their sides' and when the creatures were borne above the earth, the wheels were borne too."

The thrones are said to reside either in the third or the fourth heaven. They are said to inhabit a region in which Heaven meets Earth."

The Knowledge of the 72 Names of God and the Angelic manifestation of those 72 Names of God is also a function of the study of time. A great Sage wrote this:

"Time was the first creation; thus, the sanctification of time is the first mitzvah [holy deed] commanded to Israel AKA The Human Diaspora."

– The Rebbe

Angels are very much an Army commanded by God. God is the architect our Spiritual DNA. Here is the Organization and Duty Chart for the Angel Hierarchy. Your Guardian Angels will belong to various Hierarchies. Remember in essence the level of hierarchy is not important. The work of an Angel of the Third Hierarchy, who are closest to Realm of Humankind are no less important than the work of a Seraphim Angel of the First Hierarchy, those who sit closest to God in that Holy Realm. All are commanded to do God's work for particular reasons, to bestow attributes, give specific messages or create actions to the receiver of that attribute, action or message.

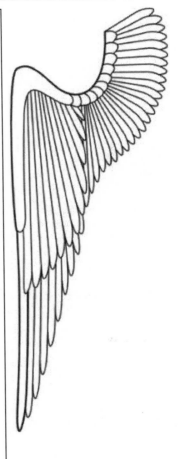

<u>Dedication</u>

Firstly, I give thanks to God for granting me the opportunity to be the vehicle to reveal the Secret of the Angel Code and my three Guardian Angels who messengered to me my spritual mission.

Then to Dr. Dennis Takarinda and Mrs. Rudo Lydia Nyamuswa for everything and all. To my sister Mabel Menaniseyi Marilyn and my brother Gilbert Mudiwa, I wouldn't be alive today without you all. In those happy and scary spaces where I knew I could share it all with you. For your unconditional love and support in ALL ways and always, if the world could only know how deeply I thank you—my family, my life. And to my nephew Tawana Dete for his beautiful Book Cover Art, I adore you.

Finally to הפזורה:

The Diaspora, the scattered, I pray may we once again be unified in the **Understanding** of of The One True G-d and **Wisdom** contained in the Orchard of The Almighty's Words. We ask of the Conductor to grant us **Mercy, Restraint,** and **Harmony** needed for the **Humility** and **Endurance** mandated by our **Connection** to the covenant with G-d. Call upon our **Receptiveness** to perform with alacrity, the *thoughts, words, and actions* that include learning the Language of G-d, follow and be guided by the statutes of the One True King. Grant us the strength to create in the **Foundation** of this world a dwelling fit for the Master of the Universe May our Saviour come soon, our Sanctury be rebuilt, and endeavor to merit our portion in The World to Come.

The Angel Hierarchy

GOD

ANGEL HEIRARCHY

First Heirarchy Angels of Pure Contemplation Govern all Creation

Seraphim Cherubim Thrones

Second Hierarchy Angels of the Cosmos Govern All Cosmos

Dominions Powers Virtues

Third Hierarchy Angels of the World Govern All the World

Principalities ArchAngels' Angels

THE ANGEL CODE
Book of Matthew Chapter 4

He shall give his angels charge concerning thee and in their hands they shall bear bear thee up, lest at any time thou dash they foot against a stone.

Psalm 91:11,12 Luke 4:10,11

Do we have Spiritual DNA? Yes we do and they are the Angels among us. We know you are out there and this book unfolds the secret of who and where the 72 Angels come from, which are coded in the Miracle Passage of the Exodus from the Torah/Bible. The Angel Code unlocks the Secret to our passions, missions and souls. Angels are spirit messengers sent to intermediate between God and humanity. They are assigned to us at birth and give us the attributes of our greatest abilities, the heights of fulfillment we can attain, contributions to our family, our community, and our World. They are sent by God to assist us. They are our personal guardians, their mission on earth to help us attain ascension to our highest Emotional, Physical and Spiritual objective. How do we tap into them, in order to prepare for a coming miracle? Each individual soul has three Guardian Angels assigned at birth. This is the technology to gain Peace of mind, Order, Peace, Love, Simplify and bring about focus on those hidden dreams or reinforce what you know you are here on this planet to do. Not only are they real, they are found in the fabric of time in the Bible. There are exactly 72 Angels derived from the Miracle Passage, Exodus 14 versus 19-21 in the Bible. Yes, they are millions upon millions, part of God's

Army, however, there are 72 main Angels governing time, space countries, and people. This book will teach you how to find your assigned Angels by their holy names from the Bible as they are assigned by time, date and place of an individual's birth, all part of a scientific "Miracle Code" of understanding the Bible as a Code of past, present and future events. This author has gone to great length and research to guide you in touching and reaching that Guardian Angel using a reproducible, mathematical formula embedded in the Bible translated from the sacred language of Aramaic. This book is the architecture of the wish fulfilled of each of us being able to realize we are meant for much greater things and great being relative, a great Mother inspiring her child, finding a cure for some dreaded illness. How do we reach them and know their manifestations and role in our everyday lives? Read the Angel Code and find your angels. This technology is for everyone and is the property of every one of us. The Angels serve dual purposes of bestowing Attributes/Characteristics and wielding Wrath/Retribution/Reckoning under the auspices of humanities covenant with G-d.

We learn to speak, read and experience a Spiritual Language, being ever closer to Diviinity, The Universe, G-d. Find your mission, Improve your life, Connect or re-connect to God. Ask and Answer Who am I? Learn to love the World, Be happy, and find Peace in your Soul. We all seek purpose and the very core of our being. I know The Angel Code, your Spiritual DNA as written in the Book of all Books we can find our vision, act on our intentions, discover the reason to commit to find our individual excellence and the integrity that is truly God given and scientific.

I remember something said by Nell Irvin Painter, she said she was making an appeal for writing/journalism in the academic genre. She said in a nutshell, we need to experience the world as an academician would. Which is research, therorems, conclusions, nuanced patterns of thought. We need to do away with opinions made on sound bites. To me sitting here really overwhelmed in producing this scientific, metaphysical and suprarational guide book, watching her on Booktv-C Span, it all came home. When you hear a truth and know the truth, that is divine. On this Christmas Day, I felt there is more redeeming value to this Holiday, to the hyper pomp, circumstance and bald-faced consumerism, and where would I get the grain of "spirit". Aside my from my family which was a non-stop theme of grace, I needed no holiday or gathering for me to be grateful. What was the point of this day, outside of religious dogma? I was disillusioned. One thing, I knew this body of work about Angels was a Divine assignment. My task now was to complete it and publish it. With about 20 Agent rejections and counting, I was losing my will. However, seeing Dr. Painter convinced me, at the very least I had taken on a true academic endeavour. That was enough, I knew I trusted in God, right then and there to get me through this desert of emotion, will and hopelessness.

So the Angel Code are the 72 thought patterns we, as people, should practice everyday. I think everyone gets up to start their day with the banal tasks. I will do 30 minutes of exercise, I will get dressed, how is traffic, how do I feel, etc. In addition to that I submit Angelogy as a mental construct to which we conduct our daily living. The 72 Angels to me suggest 72 patterns of thought and reflection we all should engage in. 72 individual characteristics of God embedded within Angels. For example, our very first Angel in the hierarchy, is Vehuiah, the Angel of Redemption and Forgiveness. This suggests the supreme attribute is Redemption and Forgiveness; for ourselves and others. Further, what does that characteristic lead us to do? The notion is the very thought pattern that Angel invokes is also most likely to create in us actions which reflects that. The academics and science of Angels in soul resonation is profound. Whatever an individual may do that day, for example under the influence of the Angel Vehuiah such as forgiveness of a co-worker because you were focused on this Angel pattern can create a butterfly effect of true profoundness. And I think we have all experienced or read stories of people who have done just that with enormous beneficial outcomes.

Within The Angel Code we merge Science and Spirituality. Not an arbitrary name plucked from nothingness, but exactly the Names, Atrributes of Guardian Angels from the Bible in the most Ancient text. Thus, there is no misinterpretation and The Angel Code is supported by the veracity of the Miracle Passage.

Your parentage, or lack of, your current state of who you are to your very core is answered in these pages. You need look no further than your Guardian Angels who ordain your attributes at their highest level for you to fulfill and enjoy. This is an eternal hope and happiness that is unlocked and is yours to experience. Better yet, since Guardian Angels are inherently Universal, use this book to connect with the Guardian Angel of the month, day or hour as a daily mediation and to receive strength and purpose.

Remember your Angels are; Messengers, Healers, Miracle workers; they can talk to God for you and remember are not to be worshipped only God is.

TABLE OF CONTENTS

CHAPTER ONE

Unlock the Secret of your Spiritual DNA

Everyone one day asks that question why am I
here? Or you wonder the place where I am right
now does not feel right—or feels so right? You
may wonder have I used my abilities to their highest
potential. What are those abilities? The Angel
Code a scientific derivation of real Angel names
and attributes may help you answer those questions
about your Spiritual DNA. Let me offer you some
states of spirit and mind; Happiness, Joy,
Prosperity, Peace of Mind, Wisdom, Freedom,
Enlightenment, Purpose. If you want any or all of
these this book through assisting you to find your
Angel Guardians as aspects of God are attainable
and exist here and now. We can recapture the
"Light" through the science of the Bible revealing
our Angels and their Ancient Names as written in
the Bible.

Everyone come into this world ushered by three
Guardian Angels assigned by God. The Bible
deciphered as the ultimate Code and Guide for life

has a special "Miracle Passage" that and that passage decoded in the ancient language from the ancient alphabet will allow you to determine those Angels. It will teach you how to identify your Spiritual, Emotional and Physical Angel. Each governing and giving you the God attributes that you are born with.

Does your Spiritual DNA include Archangel, the warrior's of God's army, maybe you're supposed to be a colonel or police chief. Do you have Angel Spiritual DNA from the Angelic Heirarchy, who are direct messengers for God who sit closest to Humanity, are you guided to be a messenger, your destiny to speak to millions about meaning of life, are you gifted with healing, you're supposed to be a doctor. Are you gifted with song, you're a great singer?

All these questions can be answered and explored in these pages. If you're not fulfilled this may give you insight to where you light shines—the most positive of your God-given traits as signified by your three Guardian Angels.

If you're troubled you speak to God through them in their Holy Names and ask them to channel to you, your highest ambition or dream. Or if you are new parents, explore the Guardian's your baby was born with, why not start to develop he or she's God given attributes inherent in their nature. The very fact you are looking at this book may mean it's time to scientifically, as written in the Ancient Book of all Books explore, understand, reach out to where your life path is, has and will lead you. This study also generates a cosmic or rather metaphysical shift and lift in your consciousness and awareness of yourself, those around you and a Higher Power.

What I Learned from the Study of Angels

I wrote this book for the hopeless, the hopeful, the curious, heavy-hearted and the overburdened. Through this journey many revelations came to pass, all leading me to a place where it was safe to be me fortes and flaws. The license to know my constant search for perfection was noble, but had to be tempered with tenderness for myself. When my mother and father died, I questioned why we even bothered living. I considered them to be the two greatest heroes in my life. Two Africans, coming from an extraordinary setting in Zimbabwe from good families to become a doctorate graduate, and masters graduate in psychiatric nursing. I knew in my genes had been the code to try harder, and explore the meaning of life. But I also was confused, why these two champions were taken away from me so early. One thing I realized is that we are born in this world as lone being, but not alone. The very fact you are taking a breath right now is because The Eternal (Ain Sof), G-d, wished it so. The possibility of a gestating unborn to realize life is perilous. So if you're here, you're meant to be, but for what?

I couldn't wrap my hand around true happiness. When I thought for a moment maybe I was turning the corner, something always came along to throw up a brick wall in front of me. I had to find someway to survive. But why? Why? It hurt me deeply flailing around life this way. Not really feeling I was fulfilling my destiny in this life, but afraid to die. I was afraid to my core I may have been hardwired for grief and tragedy. My accomplishments included a lot of things, but with those accomplishments came tragedies and they always seemed so hopelessly intertwined. And quite honestly I wrote this book because I thought if I could decode the secrets held in the meaning of life, I could save myself and understand the World. I started with the Bible. Our world was dying, from Aids, from grief, from depression, from drugs, from racism, from hate from obesity and many other big name ailments. It seemed the people I worked with at my jobs were pedantic, jealous, joyless, uncreative, unworthy, mean and hostile.

They were a few who had vision, however, many times to walk into work was a challenge. I occasionally resorted to prescriptions to alleviate my insomnia due to anxiety, and my dread. I figured if I could just keep working to pay the bills, until I equalized--I might make it. When I began to study the code of Angels it became my sanctuary. Every Angel was a positive message and trait I could re-wire my psyche with and if it helped me, maybe I could help all the other billions of people in need, who were curious, scared and change those that hateful, spiteful, unfulfilled, and uninitiated to embrace the bigger, beautiful picture of life.

I will be boastful enough to say if I could save myself with all I had been through, I could offer some solace to the greater world too. Working with Angels is like; for example, say you need to talk to the head honcho of some corporation. You can call directly but let's say you know the boss' assistant very well, and you say to the assistant, I need to talk to the boss about a certain issue. This is a very efficient assistant who is in constant communication with the boss and either makes an appointment or relays and sends you back a message. The same type of dynamic exists with Angels. They are also beings that assist in realizing what your mission is here on earth and at the very least what your particular strengths are and know they are there to assist you in your life journey. Every person should know what that mission is and make a concentrated effort in this life time to know this. This creates the most efficient aware, conscious types of humanity.

Angels also act as a finely tuned antenna to God. Knowing your mission, and that you can ask for a miracle, strength and answers through Angels is an imperative for real self-sufficiency. No father, brother, mother, sister, husband, or wife can give you that. You dwell in your mind alone, that's scary, so who can I run to when I am in need? How do I make sense of this world, how do I recognize a sign when it is given to me?

And as I was studying these questions through reading, and research, I came upon the code of Angels written in the Bible decoded from one of the most ancient of languages of mankind, Hebrew. Hebrew is a Semetic language of the Afro-Asiatic family and most interestingly considered a numerical/mathematical/symbolic language that can be used to interpret the Bible as a code for past, present and future events.

There are many schools of thought about how many Angels we are each born with. I subscribe to Three, your Emotional, Physical and Spiritual Angel. There in lies our hardwired spiritual DNA represented by our Guardian Angels that express our inherent God given strengths and path ways in life.

The Angel assignments are scientifically and mathematically derived by your date, time, place and year of birth. These calculations are precise and can be done by an individual, however for in depth analysis an individual trained in Angel decoding is beneficial, because it is a practiced science and multi-faceted in it's analysis. I am an Angel Reader.

The Miracle Code of Angels

What has been hard-wired into your Spiritual DNA? Will you be destined to be a financial guru or compose the greatest book ever written? Will you design clothing so beautiful the world has never seen? Will you usher peace between the great lands of the Earth, will you say something to a co-worker that keeps them from reaching a depth of despair so deep—you save one life in your lifetime? What are you hardwired for from the day you were born. Do you know? Do you care? Do you know you are supposed to participate in the fabric of time past, present and future as destined by God, the Almighty, The one True King, Allah--all names of the Creator messengered--through the Angels assigned to you on your Birth Day. Angels, through the Creator are manifestations of the aspects of

Godly attributes, give you insight into your destiny your full providence and a window to that place in the world where you belong. Understanding their signs can also give you protection, answers, warnings, strengths when you need it most. And what is most glorious is every one of us on this planet has three assigned Guardian Angels; who usher us into this world, talismen—we are all equal in our ability to do and feel wondrous things. This is a scientific work—the study of Angels and the ability to calculate mathematically those Angels is precision work taken straight from the Bible under the auspices of the Bible Code written as a numerical system connected to symbolic meaning.

This Book is all about the knowledge of the government of God by Angels, which the Scripture callS watchmen; and to understand the mystery of Angels.

As we examine The Names of G-d/Angels we will see H "hei" in the majority of the Names. Hei alludes to the five organs of verbal articulation, i.e., the larynx, palate, tongue, teeth and lips, which are the source of the letters אתה. Which means the phrase, "and You (אתה) give life to them all." The word אתה ("You") indicates all the letters from alef, the first letter of the Hebrew alphabet, to tav, the final letter of the alphabet,

This, then, is the The spiritual letters that emanate from the five supernal organs of verbal speech, provide life ex nihilo to the whole of the created universe. Which is the letter Hei (H).

וההי"א היא ה׳ מוצאות הפה, מקור האותיות

And the Hei (or letter H) is the source of the mouth, the source of the letters

Here we will understand the Choir of Angels, arranged in hierarchic order. They are:

1. Seraphim
2. Cherubim
3. Thrones
4. Dominions
5. Virtues
6. Powers
7. Principalities

8. Archangels
9. Angels

These nine choirs are divided into three orders. The first three are the closest to God and are sometimes called Counselors. The middle three are sometimes called Rulers because their names indicate a certain governing power. The last three are spoken of as Workers, God's messengers, and among them are the guardian Angels.

What is the Angel Code?

The Angel Code is extrapolated from the Bible in Exodus 14 vs. 19-21, the section of the bible designated as the Miracle Passage when the Israelites were saved from Pharaoh by Angelic messages from God and the Miracle of the parting of the Red Sea.

This book is for seekers. There are over a billion Angels. In Daniel 7:10 "A fiery stream issued And came forth from before Him. A thousand thousands ministered to Him; Ten thousand times ten thousand stood before Him."

Revelation 5:11 "Then I looked, and heard the voice of many angels around the throne, the living creatures, and the elders; and the number of them was ten thousand times ten thousand, and thousands of thousands."

There are 72 Main Angels this book will chronicle as deciphered from Exodus 14 vs. 19-21 in a mathematical methodology from the ancient language of Hebrew.

Why Hebrew? The Bible was written in ancient text which included Amharic, Hebrew and Arabic. All are of Afro-Asiatic Roots in their antiquity and Hebrew is a Semetic language of Afro-Asiatic origin and over time it has been the genesis of various languages all over the word. It is also one of the most original languages of the writings of the Bible. The majority of the Hebraic Bible is devoid of incorrect translation which has quite often mistranslated and distorted of it's true meaning.

What Are Bible Codes?

The Bible Codes are perhaps the most compelling enigma in history. Within the past four years several best-selling books have claimed that Bible codes about 20th Century people and events were intentionally embedded in the Hebrew Bible when it was written many centuries ago.

The best known of these books are The Bible Code (Michael Drosnin), Cracking the Bible Code (Jeffrey Satinover, M.D.) and The Signature of God, The Handwriting of God and The Mysterious Bible Codes (all by Grant Jeffrey). A **Bible code** (also **Torah code**) is the notion that there are information patterns encrypted or coded form in the text of the Bible, or, more specifically, in the Torah, the first five books of the Hebrew Bible.

Bible code research is said to date back to at least the 12th century, when rabbinical scholars first wrote about discovering meaningful words hidden in the Hebrew text of the Torah.

Tradition among the most devout religious scholars holds that everything and everyone that ever was or ever will be was recorded in the text of the first five books of the Bible. Thus, as it was passed down letter by letter from God to Moses, then generation by generation to modern times, great care has been taken to preserve it intact. Rabbis encouraged caution in Torah copyists by reminding them that just one letter lost in their work could bring about the end of the world.

Only very slight changes have occurred in the original text over the 3,200 years since Moses first received it – a wonder that ranks among the great miracles of the ages.

The existence of such codes has been hypothesized by students of Kabbalah since the Middle Ages

This book relatingThe Science of Angels or **The Angel Code: The Secret of your Spiritual DNA** is a spiritual/metaphysical science book in the methodology of books such as a **Brand New Earth** by Ekhart Tolle. It also has analytical, predictive and sacred principles of Zodiac, astrology, and characteristic horoscopes. It is the understanding and explanation of Angelic Science as a way to reveal and discover your own personal Spiritual DNA. **The Angel Code** seeks to explain how the 72 Guardian Angels derived from the Miracle Passage of the Bible connects the bridge of the scientific and spiritual on how we understand events and our surroundings. This code represented in the 72

Angel Names, also derivative of the 72 Names of God are the magnifying glass we use to experience our world in a more personally significant fashion.

The Angel Code addresses the Spiritual Frequency and Protective Quality of Angels, beyond fad, but as a Science. Angelogy supports that at the very least if what you think about is your reality, understanding Angel Science on a deeper level forces you to think on an Attraction level of what is a meaningful and positive reality. For example, the 46th Angel is named Ariel who is the Angel of Revelation. Speaking the name, thinking and addressing the authority of this Angel manifests the thought pattern of what Revelations am I experiencing in this moment that I am spiritually attuned to?

I am an Angel Scientist/Reader who subscribes to the school of thought that the Bible is a Mathematical Code, particularly when deciphered in the Ancient languages such as Aramaic and Hebrew. By understanding and deciphering this code, one can chart, the three Guardian Angels that usher you into this world. Everyone is born with three Guardian Angels assigned at birth to usher them into the world. These Angels represent our Spiritual DNA and are there to be tapped into to reach our highest potential. The Angel Code can answer these questions and more.

The Angel Code, simply put is your Spiritual DNA and is an ancient technology that reveals your individual motivations, gifts and attributes. The Angel Code asks and answers; Are you living your dreams, your passions, do you have hidden gifts that can be unlocked by knowing the Guardian Angels God has gifted you with? Yes you can.

The other point of understanding The Angel Code is learning the 72 names of the Guardian Angels, even if you do not pronounce them absolutely correctly seeing and sounding the names reverberate a positive vibration on the molecular/DNA level. It's much the same feeling when you hear or see the word "snake" as opposed to "love". Feel the difference? My work and research is to provide you with the Biblical name of those Guardian Angels by charting a person's date, time and place of birth, it's very specific and scientific. There are millions upon millions of Angels however, scientifically there are 72 Guardian Angels derived from the Miracle Passage in Exodus Chapter 14 versus 19-21. This is where the Angels appeared commanded by God, the parting of the Red Sea and deliverance from bondage. When these verses are read in Hebrew and then put in a grid you then obtain the 72 names of the Angels each representing the different attributes of your Spiritual DNA, I call the Angel Code.

While you are born with three Guardian Angels specific to you, all Angels are there for you to tap into. They are our collective Army from God. The Angel Code will guide you to which Angels govern certain attributes, Abundance, Love, Miracles and can be used as daily meditations to improve and enhance our lives.

Another provocative aspect of this book is the description of the physical manifestations of Angels. While many have the generic image of Cherubs and Ethereal women, The nine ranks of Angels as described in the Bible and ancient texts present a more complex, sometimes fearsome and otherworldly description of them. A lot like when you see the creatures that exist in the deepest oceans, strange eyes, lighted appendages because they live in a realm of their own. The same with Angels. The popular culture description of Angels neglects the biblical description of Angels, created by God and live in various levels of "Heaven". They could not possibly adhere to the popular, simplistic, unresearched descriptions of Angels. The Angel Code scientifically describes what Angels really look like and more; giving accurate descriptions of these formidable and fearsome creations. For example, the Rank of Throne Angels, whom sit closest to God are described as:

<u>The Angel Code</u> defines the days of the month, times that Angels govern. For example, let's say someone born on February 7, 19XX will possess three Guardian Angels, one that governs the Physical Realm, our material world, Our Emotional Realm, our emotional attributes and our Spiritual Realm, or spiritual imprint.

They have a distinct Organization and Duty Chart known as the Angel Hierarchy. Your Guardian Angels will belong to various Hierarchies. Remember in essence the level of hierarchy is not important. The work of an Angel of the Third Hierarchy, who are closest to Realm of Humankind are no less important than the work of a Seraphim Angel of the First Hierarchy, those who sit closest to God in that Holy Realm. All are commanded to do God's work for particular reasons, to bestow attributes, give specific messages or create actions to the receiver of that attribute, action or message.

This book is divided in three main sections. First, the days of months are referenced to the Angel who Guards that day on a physical, emotional or spiritual realm. The main part of the book is broken out by the Physical Angel. So for example, on February 3rd to the 7th, the Angel in charge is: **Mehiel**, the 64th Angel, an Archangel whom protects against adversity and is an agent of Literature. Mehiel is also the Heart of the World, and he is the catalyst like a beating heart that energizes all things. That Angel will Guard that period of time and if it falls on your birthday will be an aspect of your Spiritual DNA. The Physical and Emotional Angels are easily applied because you only need the month and day, for example, Feb 7th. The Spiritual Angel requires you know the location and time of your birth and is then translated to (Greenwich Mean Time) GMT to identify the Ruling Angel at that time. The author generally does this as a consultation due to the more intricate calculation. You may contact her at SpiritualDNA72@outlook.com for Angel Reading consultations.

Some of the things this book will enable you to do is focus. At first reading, you take in all the new information about REAL Angels. You then are able to break down the portions that really resonate with you. When you are using the book at it's most optimum level, you are using it as a daily meditation and tapping into a higher frequency or power. You are using it in times of need to get you through a hard task, difficult times or to understand gratitude for good fortune and funnel more good fortune towards you. You are making an evolutionary shift, mentally, physically and emotionally. You start to reduce your need for Doctors, pills, mind-numbing activities that do not enhance your inner self. The ability to see, understand and speak the Angels names are a huge healing on the molecular level. We all want and desire more fun for ourselves, approaching and living our life's destiny and work.

CHAPTER TWO

How to use this Book

The Angel Code should be used as a daily meditation. Each day of the month has a particular Angel that governs our physical world. In this book you will look up those days, learn about the Guardian Angel who governs that day and use that as a daily connection with God, look for "Angel signs" for that Guardian. It will contain a special meaning to each of us. Look at the name, perfect pronunciation is not necessary as seeing and absorbing the named brings about beneficial cellular and DNA changes. As I said before Angels rule on a daily, monthly, and minute-by-minute basis. They are pulling double and triple shifts. So it is also correct to call on a particular Guardian Angel which governs the attributes for Angel rescue if you will. The Physical Guardian Angel which possesses your birthday will hold special meaning and power for you. If you would like to go deeper into learning all Three of the Guardian Angels that watch over you, you can also look up which of the 72 are governing the Emotional and Spiritual Realm to get a full Angel picture of that moment.

The first you thing you may want to do is go to the index and see all the life situations Angels govern and can assist you in. Are you facing fears, new challenges or need support in a particular area? This is because while we have three specifically appointed Angels, all are available to us for guidance, support and love.

The next thing is to chart your spiritual, emotional and physical Angels according the time, day, month and year you were born and see your specific attributes.

You should read your assigned Angel attributes several times to really understand what they mean to you and hard-wire these aspects into your mind so you may call upon them at any time. You must keep in mind Angel work is a continuous process the more you work with them, the better you become at working with them. Sometimes it takes time to digest what you are reading, but perserverence and openness to the process is important.

Another note, pronouncing these Ancient names is easier for some, harder for others. The most important thing is to pronounce it as well as you can, let The Name reverberate in your mind and know that is more than enough to reap all the benefits of our Guardian Angels.

What is Angel Consciousness

An Angel is a superior state of consciousness which represents qualities and virtues of God in their essence and original conception. The mission of human beings is to rediscover them, to reprogram them in their thoughts, feelings and actions.

Angelology is represents the seventy-two states of consciousness in the form of angelic energies. When a human being works on integrating and becoming these energies, the door of true Knowledge opens:

1. Awareness of one's being through inner transformation;
2. Opening of the subconscious and unconscious;
3. Gradual interpretation and understanding of dreams, everyday signs and symbols;
4. Increased understanding of the invisible worlds and the many mysteries of the Universe.

Each Angel has a mystical Hebrew name, which evokes a vibratory echo that acts directly on the cellular memory. Each Angel also has a number - from 1 to 72 - which situates it in the celestial hierarchy.

By invoking, or repeating the sacred formula represented by the Angel's name, we create a passage between the conscious, the subconscious and the different layers of the unconscious, thus reprogramming the different angelic states of consciousness within, and allowing ourselves to reconnect with our celestial origin. The objective of this work is to purify our soul and become totally conscious in order to rediscover the Knowledge that lies within.

The Angelic Alphabet

The Hebrew 'aleph-beit' is a 'cognitive entheogen'. *[**Entheogen**: God within; god- or spirit-facilitating, a psychoactive sacramental; a plant or chemical substance taken to occasion primary religious experience. Example: peyote cactus as used in the Native American Church.]* and is divine in nature. It accurately represents ways of knowing which conserve their not-entirely-human origins, and is a living artifact from a vast Epic of adventures with celestial presence on Earth. If we look at this from the perspective of spirituality, this language is a gift to the people of Earth from our spiritual progenitors. It is also a lot like a science-fiction toy from the future — it has trans-temporal connectivities and thus comprises something of a 'prophecy device'. Hebrew is a *living* doorway to the 'outside' of what we understand as Time. I state this not as theory or philosophy but as easily demonstrated fact.

Theopoetic in function and purpose, the whole of creation is experienced by initiates as encoded in a magical way in the archetypal identities, shapes, histories, and relations of the letters. These relations are commonly non-linear, and so potentially diverse as to defy any single system of exploration. Each entity in a letter, word or phrase is reflectively redefined by systems of context, position and a magically-founded numerism which is most likely the source of modern 'numerology'.

The 613 thousand letters of the Torah are said to comprise a single name of God, and a remembrance of the number of the souls who departed Egypt during Exodus. But hidden within the relational symmetries of the letters are profound doorways to ecstatic communion with their source. For thousands of years the 'hidden' aspects of Hebrew have escaped secular understanding almost entirely — a common goal of any sacred tongue. Yet these matters and ways are not meant to remain *forever* hidden, and in truth we live in a new Eon where

what was long hidden is now to be revealed and
magnified in our lives and experience — not merely
in books.

Whether or not Hebrew is 'the chosen language' is
a question for those children *who prefer division to
unity*, so too are questions relating to authorization
to know, use or learn it. Hebrew is an amazing
archeocognitive enlightenment tool and its purpose
is liberation, not admonition and wrathful judgment
as we are too often convinced by those who know
too little of these matters to have any reasonable
credentials for 'teaching us' of them.

CHAPTER THREE

The Angelic Alphabet Explained

The Angelic Alphabet is also the Hebrew Alphabet,
a sacred text where meaning is derived unedited,
and untranslated as in mistranslated. Each alphabet
has a meaning and numerical value, so when you
decode the Miracle passage and derive each letter
name of an Angel the result is a number and
meaning and Godly attribute of that Angel and

further becomes your number, meaning and attribute. See Table 6.

For Example, You read Hebrew from right to left. For example the Angel, the Archangel Michael:

M = Mem מ   Water
I/Y = Yud י   Hand of God
C = Kaf כ   A bent crown, humility, wing
H = Hei   ה   Window, lattice, Breathe of God
L = Lamed ל   Corrrection, learning, teaching
                        by God

Here you see the words water, hand, humility, window, and correction/learning. Water biblically is life/knowledge/the Torah (all agents of "knowledge"), hand (of God) mercy, humility, correction/learning as in learning something like truths? What is concealed?

Michael, number 42, is the Archangel described as "Similar to God" and "The Right Hand of God", which is Mercy. This Angel rules over Wednesday. He reveals the concealed, just as the Creator's truths are often concealed before they are revealed and it

is up to the individual to discover those truths.
Those born under this Angel have the attributes of
revealing what is concealed. They make good
diplomats, Secretary of States and protectors of the
state and revealing of that which is wrong with the
state as identified as a entity or person. From the
macro to the micro level.

Another interesting thing is you may also use this
code in deciphering your own name, for according
to Bible science, every event is pre-ordained so
your name is not random, your family is not
random—so the pursuit of breaking out these
meanings can be revelations. Let's try an example.
My name given at birth by my parents is Sarah.
(See Table 1)

S	Shin	A year; change; a tooth; scarlet; serenity; to sleep; to teach; two; sharp; old; viceroy.	300
R	Reish	Head	200
H	Hei	Window, network or door, Breathe of God which created the Aleph-Beit	5

The Numerical total of Sarah is 505, you must then
reduce it to 55, a double digit representation of the
letter H or Hei, which inherently alludes to

windows/light/the introduction to prophecy, just as Sarah was in the Bible. You also may then reduce 55 to add those number to get 10, then reduce down to 1+0 = 1. 1 equals A, aleph, God, Sarah is a prophetic window to God.

In most instances when you get a double digit (power number) you do not add further.

So Sarah is a 1 numerically. The number 1 is a doorway or gateway into your highest potential as a human seeking divine memory. One is a singularity within 'all that is'. The 'one' seeks itself through a mirror like reflection of the world around it. This doorway offers an opportunity to surpass any limitations you have unknowingly set for yourself. One to one to one enter the oneness hidden deep within your being at the center point of your soul.

The symbolic meaning of Sarah has some nuances as understood from the Hebrew alphabet. She is part of the Beginning of Creation. Sarah, considered a prophetess, biblically was the wife of Abraham and is first mentioned in Genesis, when the world was created, she is also a window someone who provides clarity for others "sort of a window to souls" and also reflects back to herself as a window you may look out of and into. Within the name Sarah exists the eternal flame, the act of clarification, and expression in speech, thought and action. These are some of the interpretation divined from this name.

If I were to describe myself it would be a person who looks for patterns, networks, doors into the psyche of the world and cosmos. I'm a mirror/window looking deep within and out. I've always been someone who creates—always at the Beginning of new thought, new ideas, birthing of new "life" and also looking back deep into my/our past for answers for now and tomorrow. To me, my name is no coincidence. I see myself as one who supports Gods in disseminating the knowledge of Angels, and ancient wisdom so we may to get closer to God for all of humankind.

Chart 8 will assist you in the mathematical/numerical/symbolic mechanics of Deriving Angels for individuals from the Bible. This identifies their names and symbolic meanings.

First, we will be using Hebrew primarily because it is one of the most Ancient languages the Bible was written in it's most original text. The Hebrew Alphabet a precursor to the current alphabet has meanings within meanings assigned to each letter describing our relationship to the Creator and they also had numerical values. Numerology is tied to Angel reading in that when an individual experiences a number on a clock radio, a license plate on tv they can be attributed to Angel signs. Here you will not only be able to derive your Guardian Angels but understand in every breath, moment we live we are in constant communication with the Creator through Angelic messages. Conversely as messages are given to us, we may request of them almost anything.

This passage from Zohar Vayikra 1450 from Aleph to Tav reading for 3/1/14

"וַיִּקְרָא, אֶל-מֹשֶׁה; וַיְדַבֵּר יְהוָה אֵלָיו, מֵאֹהֶל מוֹעֵד לֵאמֹר."
The words mean, "And YHVH called unto Moses, and spoke unto him out of the tent of meeting, saying:"

There are five books that make up the Torah. The number five in Kabbalah represents the Ten Sefirot as Keter, Chokmah, Binah, Zeir Anpin (six Sefirot) and Malchut. The first book, "בראשית" (Genesis) is Keter, "שמות" (Exodus) is Chokmah, "ויקרא" (Leviticus) is Binah, "במדבר" (Numbers) is Zeir Anpin and "דברים" (Deuteronomy) is Malchut.

The process of transformation from Spiritual to Physical is called "השתלשלות", evolving. Keter is the connecting point to the Endless and the source of the light, Chokmah, channels the light and Binah begins the process of manifestation or the forming of the vessel. (To simplify, vessel is a container of light with ability to create or cause an action in this world).

The book of Genesis, Beresheit in Hebrew, is the source of everything in this world. Exodus (Shemot) which is the specific book of that contains The 72 Names of God, The Miracle/Angel Code, brings the revelation of the light through the process and the miracles of breaking the bondage to Egypt, the revelation on Mount Sinai and the completion of building the Tabernacle.

In Leviticus (Vayikra) we have the tools to activate and use the light. The first verse "ויקרא־אל־משה" with small א Aleph initiates the connection of the Light through the Tabernacle and the Torah as "לוחות־העדות", the Tablets is in the Arc. Rabbi Yosef Gikatilla in "Gates of Lights" "שערי אורה" explains that the Aleph is for Ohel Moed "אוהל־מועד", 'Tent of Meeting'. The call to Moshe from Ohel Moed is a connection of the Light from the level of Malchut, represented by the letter Alef.

The Zohar begins the portion with Rabbi Elazar quoting Isaiah the prophet saying to king Ahaz, Isaiah 7:11

"שְׁאַל־לְךָ אוֹת, מֵעִם יְהוָה אֱלֹהֶיךָ; הַעְמֵק שְׁאָלָה, אוֹ הַגְבֵּהַּ לְמָעְלָה."

"'Ask thee a sign (Letter) from YHVH your God: ask it either in the depth, or in the height above.'"

The Zohar then asks the question "What's the difference between the first and the last generations?" and answers that the first generations knew the supernal wisdom of the letters and how to combine them into powerful tools to control actions in this world. Even the wicked ones in Israel, Like King Ahaz knew the letters of Binah and the Letters of Malchut.

The Hebrew letters are vessels for the light. They come to this world from Binah, processed through Zeir Anpin and manifest in Malchut.
The letters were given to Moses on Mount Sinai that brought them down to us with all their possible light concealed in the Torah.

The only way to connect to the higher spiritual levels is through the study and use of the Hebrew letters. Zohar Vayikra contains many names of angels. Their names represent spiritual forces. If we remove, add, or change any letters in their name, they will no longer be who they are. Each letter in their name is like a chemical agent in a complex formula. All angels' names end with the letters el= אל or ah=אה that gives them the ability to pass between the lower and upper world.

There are 16 occurrences in the Torah with different size letters. Ten large letters connect us to the level of Binah and six small letters connect us to Malchut of Zeir Anpin.

The first letter of the Torah is the letter "ב" of "בראשית" Beresheit or B. It signifies that the seed of the Torah is in Binah "Understanding". That is where the energy comes to Zeir Anpin (The Torah). The first verse of the Torah says " בְּרֵאשִׁית, בָּרָא אֱלֹהִים, אֵת " , "In the beginning/the coming of Creation (not in the beginning God created) '."'את אֵת , AT represent the first and last letters of the Hebrew letters. The first four letters of the Torah reveal that the first thing God created was the Hebrew letters. Only on the third verse God 'speaks'. Read "The DNA of Creation" http://dailyzohar.com/daily-zohar-1448/

These aforementioned sciences encomposs Angelogy, many teachings that are connected via the sacred alphabet, the construction of the Torah revealing the Angel Code. We are assigned Angels, but all Angels are accessible to us, especially when you know the realms they govern so one can be as specific as possible in asking for light upon a problem, a decision, an event. You may not always be told the why's that is the infinite divide of Divinity, but a better insight into these actions and possibly react better in more positive way to things we don't understand.

The names of angels reflect their official duties or roles in the cosmic schema of things; each letter shines a divine light that can be meditated upon and contemplated. Angel names are "names of power" used in prayers, incantations and on amulets to help the mortal person gain access to the mysteries expressed by the name, and also provide protection against the forces of darkness. This author utilized the derivation of their duties by the root word employed in each name of God. They also a related to the 72 names of God as Angels are aspects of God's will.

Why Use Hebrew or Archaic alphabets for Angelology? It is the Formative Hyper language of the Hebrew Alphabet of Creation

CHAPTER THREE

Also remember as we go through the 72 Name Sequence, it is important to understand that G-d created everything ex-nihilo, however continues to create in every subsequent moment to sustain creation of this world. The Miracle Passage is a profound hypertext sequence that manifests this phenomena. The East wind is called to part the Red Sea, the diaspora is constantly being "embedded" with feelings, information, acts of concealment and revelation are being communicated, each an important action to create, actualize and complete a process that fulfills the archetypical blueprint. The resulting manifestation, Divinely whole.

One should also reference Psalm 106 that encapsulates the journey and tone of the Miracle Passage.

"Psalms Chapter 106

The psalmist continues the theme of the previous psalm, praising God for performing other miracles not mentioned previously, for "who can recount the mighty acts of God?" Were we to try, we could not mention them all!

1. Praise the Lord! Praise the Lord for He is good, for His kindness is everlasting.

2. Who can recount the mighty acts of the Lord, or proclaim all His praises?

3. Fortunate are those who preserve justice, who perform deeds of righteousness all the time.

4. Remember me, Lord, when You find favor with Your people; be mindful of me with Your deliverance;

5. to behold the prosperity of Your chosen, to rejoice in the joy of Your nation, to glory with Your inheritance.

6. We have sinned as did our fathers, we have acted perversely and wickedly.

7. Our fathers in Egypt did not contemplate Your wonders, they did not remember Your abundant kindnesses, and they rebelled by the sea, at the Sea of Reeds.

8. Yet He delivered them for the sake of His Name, to make His strength known.

9. He roared at the Sea of Reeds and it dried up; He led them through the depths, as through a desert.

10. He saved them from the hand of the enemy, and redeemed them from the hand of the foe.

11. The waters engulfed their adversaries; not one of them remained.

12. Then they believed in His words, they sang His praise.

13. They quickly forgot His deeds, they did not wait for His counsel;

14. and they lusted a craving in the desert, they tested God in the wilderness.

15. And He gave them their request, but sent emaciation into their souls.

16. They angered Moses in the camp, and Aaron, the Lord's holy one.

17. The earth opened and swallowed Dathan, and engulfed the company of Abiram;

18. and a fire burned in their assembly, a flame set the wicked ablaze.

19. They made a calf in Horeb, and bowed down to a molten image.

20. They exchanged their Glory for the likeness of a grass-eating ox.

21. They forgot God, their savior, Who had performed great deeds in Egypt,

22. wonders in the land of Ham, awesome things at the Sea of Reeds.

23. He said that He would destroy them-had not Moses His chosen one stood in the breach before Him, to turn away His wrath from destroying.

24. They despised the desirable land, they did not believe His word.

25. And they murmured in their tents, they did not heed the voice of the Lord.

26. So He raised His hand [in oath] against them, to cast them down in the wilderness,

27. to throw down their progeny among the nations, and to scatter them among the lands.

28. They joined themselves to [the idol] Baal Peor, and ate of the sacrifices to the dead;

29. they provoked Him with their doings, and a plague broke out in their midst.

30. Then Phineas arose and executed judgement, and the plague was stayed;

31. it was accounted for him as a righteous deed, through all generations, forever.

32. They angered Him at the waters of Merivah, and Moses suffered on their account;

33. for they defied His spirit, and He pronounced [an oath] with His lips.

34. They did not destroy the nations as the Lord had instructed them;

35. rather, they mingled with the nations and learned their deeds.

36. They worshipped their idols, and they became a snare for them.

37. They sacrificed their sons and daughters to demons.

38. They spilled innocent blood, the blood of their sons and daughters whom they sacrificed to the idols of Canaan; and the land became guilty with blood.

39. They were defiled by their deeds, and went astray by their actions.

40. And the Lord's wrath blazed against His people, and He abhorred His inheritance;

41. so He delivered them into the hands of nations, and their enemies ruled them.

42. Their enemies oppressed them, and they were subdued under their hand.

43. Many times did He save them, yet they were rebellious in their counsel and were impoverished by their sins.

44. But He saw their distress, when He heard their prayer;

45. and He remembered for them His covenant and He relented, in keeping with His abounding kindness,

46. and He caused them to be treated mercifully by all their captors.

47. Deliver us, Lord our God; gather us from among the nations, that we may give thanks to Your Holy Name and glory in Your praise.

48. Blessed is the Lord, the God of Israel, forever and ever. And let all the people say, "Amen! Praise the Lord!"

CHAPTER FOUR

How Angels are Assigned from The Bible Miracle Passage

How you decipher/derive the Angel Codes. (Remember Hebrew is read right to left.

In the miracle passage in Hebrew each verse has 72 letters and when combined as 1st letter of the 1st verse, with the last letter of the 2nd verse, and the 1st letter of the third verse, in descending order creating a three letter code which are also designated as the

72 names of God, extrapolated further become the 72 names of the Guardian Angels. Coded derivatives of the miracle of the parting of the Red Sea and the role of God and Angels. See Table 1, 2, 3, 4, 5.

This is the key to the Angelic code. This mathematical grid gives you the first part of the Angel name. El, al or ah which mean of God give you the full Angel name. For example our 1st Angel is Vav Hei Vav or VHV, and "ah" and you get Vehuiah. The Holy name of the first Angel. It is also important to learn the pronunciation because the power of the spoken name. Just as one might say "love" vs. "snake". Each invokes certain feeling from the broadest level to the most deepest/spiritual, deep in the DNA of your life inward and outward. That is part of the power of The Angel Code.

CHAPTER FIVE

ANGELS OF THE MONTH

Please note, for ease of individual Angel explanation, the author uses, he, it or the Angel, for descriptive purposes, not necessarily for gender designation.

Each Angel rules for 5 days in our 360 Sacred Calendar. Note it is really the Lunar/Sacred Calender which has a lunar pattern of the number of days to a year. Some years are 355 days all the way to 385 days. They also pull double, triple, quadruple and simultaneous duty in the three Realms of our Physical, Emotional and Spiritual Worlds. These days correspond to the Ruling Physical Angel. Further in the book, I will show you how to find the ruling days for the Emotional and Physical Worlds. In the Sacred Calendar April is the 1st month.

What is important about the 22 Hebrew/Aramaic letters in the hypertext language embedded in the letters The inner meanings of the 22 letters of the Hebrew alphabet which describe different states and biological organizations of two-fold energy in its spiritual and material aspects. These are the "fundamental powers of being" (G. Scholem), or primary building blocks of creation. The first nine letters, from Aleph (1) to Tet (9) describe the formation of these completely-generalized structures, from the Intemporal to the Cell, on the level of archetype or seed. They are mirrored on the next two levels, existential (10-90) ((in opposition: their meanings are the reverse of the archetypal/seed level)) and cosmic (100-900) (in transcendence: their meanings are cosmically significant as resolutions or syntheses of the oppositions of the first two levels).

 Energy is structured in nine generalized states on three levels:
•1-9: archetypal, seed, or primitive: energies beyond our space-time continuum: Aleph to Tayt
•10-90: existential, actualized in space-time within the cone of light: Yod to Tsadde
•100-900: cosmic, beyond space-time, on the other side of the wall of light: Qof to Tsaddek.
(credit: Suarez).

The structure of the mechanics, description, sacred calendar Aramaic/Hebraic translations will be the Angel number from 1 to 72. The Name of God and it's Angelic intellence name and it's Choir and

Duty, and some with "Root Word" translations. Some names due to availability of Information will not contain all those structures, however still provide the God Name/Angelic Intelligence influence in time, planets, space, meaning and suprarational interpretation. Remember, the more you work with these Names, the easier it becomes to internalize and utilize them to their greatest good and potential in your physical and metaphysical world. Not only as a science, but a way of soul resonation, way of life, meditational and invocation properties which the benefits are of infinite breadth and depth. You tap into the omnipresence, omnipotence of knowing the Holy Language of God. Please note any Angels that do not contain the Hebrew Letters in their description please reference Table 1 and 5 for their full Hebrew/Aramaic spellings.

Lunar/Sacred Calendar NISSAN 1 to 6
Approximately: March 20 – March 24 of ARIES

1.   Vav Hei Vav OR VHV

וֵהַו

(read from left to right Vav Hei Vav)

6 + 5 + 6 = 8 is Gematria/Numerical value
Angel Order: Seraphim
Angelic Name: Vehuiah; "The Rescue and Deliver Angel"
These three letters have multiple connotations. Among them are; rescue, deliver, redeem as well as "extend, [a] hand, reach stretch. This is the first sequence of the first Name of G-d in the "Miracle Passage of Exodus". Here Moses is instructed to stretch out his hand to part the Red Sea. Thereby the rescuing and delivering the Exodus from Pharoah.

Important to note that "Hei" is the breath of G-d. In metaphysical terms the voice of G-d is thunder, howling winds, rumbling, sounds that pierce the air. In physics many of you have seen operatic singers who break glasses with the sound of their voice and sonic booms that can shatter material. This is the same principle of the mechanics of the parting of the Red Sea.

Attributes/Meditations: This Name/Angel technology is for rescue and repair our transgressions. As the first Name it is supreme and the Ruling Name/Angel to clear the path for the "great escape" our sins. His attribute is interpreted as God elevated and exalted above all things. He is a supreme ruling Angel. The person with this attribute will dominate in sciences and finance. The person who is born under the influence of this angel is joined to the window/breathe of God to commands; being blessed with great wisdom, a lover of the Arts and Sciences, capable of undertaking and executing the most difficult things; having a love for military service, due to the influence of Mars; have abundant energy, due to the dominance of fire. This Angel is related to time travel; turning back the annals of time and past sins are cleansed. Vehuiah assists us to recuperate when we are tired. This Angel facilitates the study of the scientific matters, develops in us the spirit of assertiveness and boldness. Unkind words and actions have cause and effect. The distance is metaphysical but there is sure to be an effect, a negative one, this Angel allows us to back to that time and reform that negativity.

The negative side of this angel influences turbulent men; and rules over promptness and anger.

2nd Name of G-d

MARCH 25 – MARCH 29
NISSAN 7 – 13
ARIES – Moon/Earth Position in Aries

י ל י

Yod Lamed Yod OR YLY
Angel Name: Ieliel
10 + 30 + 10 = Gematria of 5
***Wailing, howling [hurricane-force≥ 64 knot ≥**
46 ft
≥ 32.7 m/s

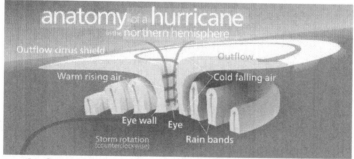

; gale-force], in meteorology . a wind of 32–63

miles per hour/about 51 to 102 kilometers per hour (14–28 m/sec). lament, "for me". This Name of G-d or Angel attribute where the mechanism of creating the forces of nature, wind force, i.e. wailing/the hurricane, where the Hand of G-d moves the Red Sea with the power of the wind.

This Angelic/God Name is creating the calm "eye" of the storm where air is pushed down towards the bed of the sea and the outer regions are in a turbulent pattern. The simultaneous calm within the storm which created the opening path for the diaspora and the turbulent walls of the displaced water.

Medititation: Calm within the storm. A person born with this Physical Guardian possesses the ability to "keep the peace" in turbulent times. As an Emotional or Spiritual manifestation the same aspect applies. Delivery into the hands of/the state of peace in turbulent times. One may also perceive that the very presence of the storm has this region of calm. The dichotomy of the

**calm against the backdrop of chaos can bring
about appreciation of the two states of existence;
i.e. without night, you wouldn't perceive day.**

**"The Peace Angel"
Vav Lamed Vav**

Type: Seraphim
Means: The Merciful Hand of God that Corrects

Attributes: One invokes this angel to obtain peace,
calm popular rabble-rousing, and to obtain victory
over those who would attack you unjustly. This
angel rules over kings and princes, and keeps their
constituency obedient; he has influence over
generations (people) and all beings that exist in the
animal realms. Jeliel establishes peace between
spouses and maintains conjugal fidelity. Those
born under this influence have a cheerful spirit,
agreeable and genteel manners; they are passionate
in sex. This Angel develops generosity, optimism
and joy in life. Jeliel supports the study of the
abstract matters and also to harmonize married life.
This Angel supports learning, correction and

lightening (to open the path to freedom), as well as "above is as below" It joins heaven and earth.

The negative side of this angel dominates everything detrimental to animate beings; it delights in distracting spouses from their duties; he inspires a taste for isolation and bad values.

3. **Sitael: "The Hope Angel"**
SYT

MARCH 30 TO APRIL 3
NISSAN 13 – 18
ARIES – Moon/Earth Position in Aries

ט י ס

Tet Yod Samech   TYS (read from left to right)

9 + 10 + 60 = Gematria of 7
**Root word: to terrify, horrify. Interpreting this
Name of G-d would inherently connote the Left
Hand of G-d; severity. Beholding the witness of
Moses' action which began the miracle process
of parting the Red Sea. This would serve to
terrify Pharoah and his Army of the one and
only G-d, and of course the fleeing diaspora
would feel the full impact of the Power, awe and
fear of G-d. Fear being an important element of
the beginning of wisdom.
Meditiation: These letters invoke the
"understanding" of G-d's unfathomable power.
How fear of G-d is a multi-facted blessing. It
overpowers your enemy for your benefit, as well**

as bring about in you this overwhelming awe of G-d's power and this is an energy you xml protocol in your being.

Type: Seraphim
Meaning: The God Mark to Protect and Surround with Mercy

Atttributes: Sitael protects against adversities. Those born under this Angel will be successful in the judicial and financial businesses. He protects against weapons and wild beasts. A person born under this influence loves truth, will keep his word, will oblige those in need of his services. He rules over nobility, magnanimity and great works; he protects against weapons/arms and ferocious beasts.

The person born under this genus will have the attributes of contributing to the study philosophy and the religions. Sitael allows us to avoid excess. Sitael develops our personality. He assists us to clear up and crystallize our destiny. Sitael contributes in amending the psychological problems related to the past.

This Angel ignites the power of miracles, by rejecting all selfishness, envy, anger and self pity.

The negative side of this angel rules hypocrisy, ingratitude and perjury.

4TH NAME
APRIL 4 TO APRIL 8
NISSAN 19 – 24
ARIES – Moon/Earth Position in Aries

Name: עלם

Ayin Lamed Mem (final Mem)
70 + 30 + 600 = Gematria of 7
Root Word: To hide, to conceal, to tie up. The action of the parting of the Red Sea which included hurricane wind, a veritable tempest, not only would conceal the fleeing diaspora, much like a parent who covers a child or loved one from harm.
Meditation: You are concealed within G-d sanctuary in times of trouble. You are cradled in the Almighty's bosom, especially when the enemy, (inclusive of those who do NOT fear G-d), seems to have surrounded you to overcome you.

Concealment is an important aspect of G-d's plan. In this excerpt of Psalm 18, it is clearly explained just how powerful it is:

Chapter 18

If one merits a public miracle, he should offer a song to God, including in his song all the miracles that have occurred since the day the world was created, as well as the good that God wrought for Israel at the giving of the Torah. And he should say: "He Who has performed these miracles, may He do with me likewise."

1. For the Conductor. By the servant of the Lord, by David, who chanted the words of this song to the Lord on the day the Lord delivered him from the hand of all his enemies, and from the hand of Saul.

2. He said, "I love You, Lord, my strength.

3. The Lord is my rock, my fortress, and my rescuer. My God is my strength in Whom I take shelter, my shield, the horn of my salvation, my stronghold.

4. With praises I call upon the Lord, and I am saved from my enemies.

5. For the pangs of death surrounded me, and torrents of evil people terrified me.

6. Pangs of the grave encompassed me; snares of death confronted me.

7. In my distress I called upon the Lord, I cried out to my God; and from His Sanctuary He heard my voice, and my supplication before Him reached His ears.

8. The earth trembled and quaked; the foundations of the mountains shook-they trembled when His wrath flared.

9. Smoke rose in His nostrils, devouring fire blazed from His mouth, and burning coals flamed forth from Him.

10. He inclined the heavens and descended, a thick cloud was beneath His feet.

11. He rode on a cherub and flew; He soared on the wings of the wind.

12. He made darkness His concealment, His surroundings His shelter-of the dense clouds with their dark waters.

13. Out of the brightness before Him, His clouds passed over, with hailstones and fiery coals.

14. The Lord thundered in heaven, the Most High gave forth His voice-hailstones and fiery coals.

15. He sent forth His arrows and scattered them; many lightnings, and confounded them.

16. The channels of water became visible, the foundations of the world were exposed-at Your rebuke, O Lord, at the blast of the breath of Your nostrils.

17. He sent from heaven and took me; He brought me out of surging waters.

18. He rescued me from my fierce enemy, and from my foes when they had become too strong for me.

19. They confronted me on the day of my misfortune, but the Lord was my support.

20. He brought me into spaciousness; He delivered me because He desires me.

4. Elemiah: "The Courage Angel"
Ayin Lamed Final Mem ALM

Type: Seraphim
Meaning: The Concealed or Hidden God
Hebraic Translation: Ayin Lamed Mem Yod Hei

Atttributes: Elemiah is deep perception, with the Eye to correct/learn and calm troubled water. Elemiah assists against spiritual torment and mental troubles. This Angel allows us to develop the spirit of initiative, courage and "the fight". It gives enthusiasm and dynamism. This Angel also assists in identifying traitors. This Angel rules over travel, maritime expeditions, and he rules over useful discoveries. The person born under its influence will be industrious, happy in his enterprises, successful and will have a passion for travel.

Elemiah assists in eliminating negative thoughts, thereby allowing light to shine through. Elemiah support us in vocational guidance and contributes to the success of our occupations. This Angel allows us to build up our physical condition and have control over aggressiveness and impulsiveness.

The negative side of this angel rules over bad education, discoveries that are dangerous to society; he also brings hindrance to all enterprises.

5th Angel: Mahasiah: "The Salvation Angel"

APRIL 9 – APRIL 13
NISSAN 23 TO NISSAN 28 5TH NAME OF G-D
LUNAR SIGN ARIES

מ ה ש

S H M
MEM HEI SHIN *(read left to right)*

300 + 5 + 40 = Gematria of 3

Attributes:
Root Words: Mem Hei; What, which, why, for what
Mem Yod Shin; to remove, to depart, to feel, touch
This Name indicates G-d's power to remove you from a situation. Here, the Exodus of removing the diaspora from slavery/bondage. This aspect is referring to water "mem", hei "curtain, also breath of G-d, and "shin"; teeth, G-d smiling upon us. It is the word of G-d, the sacred text of Torah, Old Testatment which is also considered water that nourishes and elevates the soul. Hei which is a

curtain or window, also the breath of G-d that breathed life into Adam and created the alphabet, in conjunction with shin, G-d smiling upon us is denoting G-d's comforting words to the Diaspora, encouragement to give us the strength to keep moving forward out of a dangerous situation. Meditation of this Name: The comfort and strength of G-d's words which includes studying the Torah, Old Testatment using the Orchard/PARDES of the 4 levels of understanding is the vehicle that removes us from troubling, dangerous situations. This action in itself study, learning, being receptive and following G-d's statutes is more powerful than any man, beast or entity we face.

Mem Hei Shin MHS

Type: Seraphim
Meaning: God the Purifier

Attributes: Mahasiah literally is the Angel that has the power to Purify as an entitiy of cleansing (like water and water as knowledge) and by the breathe of God allows us to "hear" that is within the 22 letters of Light (language) as in really

understanding the voice of God in whatever form is
manifests and this is the language of sound and
light.   This is the purification factor that assists us
to live in peace with everyone. He governs high
science, occult philosophy, theology, and the liberal
arts.

This Angel is associated with healing/purification of
all manner of dis-ease.

*The negative side of this angel rules ignorance, and
all bad qualities of mind and body.*

APRIL 14 – APRIL 18
IYAR 1 TO IYAR 6
6TH NAME OF G-D
LUNAR SIGN TAURUS

ללה

HLL

Lamed Lamed Hei (read right to left)
$5 + 30 + 30 = 11$ = Gematria of 11

Root Words:
To flame, to flash, to glitter. Incandescence.
Attributes/Function: This Name of G-d intimates a
luminosity and radiance. As in the power of a kind
of halo that animates as well as surrounds your
being or soul. As G-d is moving/transporting the
diaspora from a dangerous situation within a
soothing aura of light.

הָלַל halal to be clear, to shine, to make a, show, to
boast, to be, to rave, to celebrate, to stultify

Verb;
a primitive root;
Meaning: 1) to shine
1a) to shine (fig. of God's favour)
1b) to flash forth light
2) to praise
To be praised, be made praiseworthy, be
commended, be worthy of praise, glory
A protective shadow (
Meditation on this Name: G-d's infusion of
radiance that soothes, protects with a supernal light.
Note in many of the Names of G-d, H/Hei ה is used
repeatedly. The Action of the letter Hei connotes
the breath/word of G-d that permutates the Names
of G-d as well as the symbolic meaning of Hei
which is window, curtain, matrix; the very blueprint
that embeds the power of the 22 letters or alphabet
of G-d. This is the medium of understanding
biblical code, the power of language, hence the
hypertext action of the 72 Names of G-d.
Lamed or L looks like a bolt of lightening. It is the
only letter that transcends above and below
compared to the rest of the alphabet. It is almost a
direct conduit of what is "above" is also as "below".

As we go through the sequence of the Names of G-d, it creates within us that same kind of "miracle" sequence above and beyond just experiencing the Exodus as a biblical event, but also embedding this "code" within our being. It reaches levels that are deep within the sub and supra conscious.

Lelahel: "The Fame Angel"
Lamed Lamed Hei: LLH

Type: Seraphim
Meaning: The Bright God

Attributes: Lelahel dominates love, celebrity, fame and fortune and also influences the sciences and the arts. Lelahel is the flash of brightness, like fame or fortune or the flash of greatness. Here we find the power of the flash of genius, ideas and blinding light within ourselves. It is the intensity of Lamed, stressed twice within this Name of God of powerful intent to solve problems, cure illness directly from God.

The person born under this influence will love to converse, and will acquire fame through his talents and actions. The energy of intense of brightness in spirit.

The negative side of this angel rules boastfulness; he brings men to want to elevate themselves above their fellow man; he influences all those who seek to acquire a fortune through illicit means.

APRIL 19 – APRIL 23
7TH NAME OF G-D
IYAR 7 TO IYAR 12
LUNAR SIGN TAURUS

א כ א
ALEPH KAF ALEPH
A C A
1 + 20 + 1 = Gematria of 22

Root words: א כ

Words Drive away, plow, dig, palm, lure, enthrall, fascination

כ א

Words: Bend, Urge, Press, Urgency, Pressure
Attributes/Function: This Name of G-d is performing the action of urgent movement. A driving force to move something/someone forward not only using the "palm" of G-d, but also luring, enthralling the diaspora to acquiesce to this forward motion.

Meditation: At times we may be stunned into inaction by fear and uncertainty. During the Exodus the diaspora was divided in their response to Pharoah's Army. Some wanted to just walk into the Red Sea, with the thought of a mass suicide, not with the intention or belief the Sea would part. The Second group wanted to raise arms to stop to fight Pharoah. The 3rd Group wanted to sit and make lengthy praise to G-d, the 4th Group decided it was better to return to Egypt as slaves, no longer possessing the spirit to defy Pharoah. None of these decisions were according to G-d's commandment. He told Moses, tell them to just move, as soon as they step into the Red Sea, I have already delivered them, the waters will part. All the aforementioned four groups' reactions meant the forward momentum would stop, thereby defeating the purpose of this Exodus which was already promised and sanctified. This is a Name we can use to connect to the Creator to pacify and calm ourselves and to keep moving foreward despite all external phenomena that shake and destabilize our faith. We delve into a hypnotic, supernally enthralled state to press on with surety.

The negative side of this angel is the enemy of knowledge; he rules over negligence, laziness and indifference for study.

APRIL 24 – APRIL 29
8TH NAME OF G-D
IYAR 13 TO IYAR 18
LUNAR SIGN TAURUS

כ ה ת

K H T

20 + 5 + 400 = GEMATRIA OF 11

The God of Alleviation

Root Word(s): כ ה

Attributes: Aa quenching, dulling, lessening, healing, allevation, to sustain, support, nourish, restrain, endure, provide sustenance (victuals), yield to, accept.

This Name of G-d creates a state of healing, lessening "trauma". This Name also is associated with, taking a deep breath to calm in a tumultuous situation, and acquiesce. We are receiving and accepting the calm within in the storm. Diffusing anxiety and yielding enough to accept it in contentment.

Meditation: This is the spiritual SEO for diffusing the panic attack. The ancient letter sequence that equals a valium capsule. It may be we are in a swirling hurricane. Your personal Egypt a.k.a. bondage at our back and the threat of drowning in the Sea of uncertainty in front of us. With this Name we html/xml "how to diffuse overwhelming situations" via our simple faith in our Spiritual healer, G-d.

Cahetel: "The Angel who Diffuses Negative Energy"
KAF HEI TAV: KHT

Type: Seraphim
Meaning: The Miraculous God

Attributes: Cahetel allows us to obtain the blessings of God and to drive away evil spirits to bring in the Light and banish stress. He inspires humility towards God, to thank Him for all the goods He sends to earth. With this influence the humble person gains the mark of God's Light in the 22 letters of creation and Light.

The negative side of this angel provokes man to blaspheme against God. A lack of humility for blessings.

APRIL 30 – MAY 4
9th NAME OF G-D
IYAR 19 TO IYAR 24
LUNAR SIGN TAURUS

The God of Movement

Angel Haziel

ה ז י

Hei Zayin Yod
HZY
5 + 7 + 10 = Gematria of 5

Root Word(s)

Meaning: cheerfulness to dream, sleep, rave,
enthusiastic, glowing, shining, sleep
With this name we invoke brightness, splendour
And the beneficent countenance of God. We are
abundant and able to move things to into and out
of our way.
Attributes/Function: This Name bears the
power of radiance and the action of moving

things, people, creatures, etc. It is an infusion of the countenance of G-d that ignites enthusiasm, i.e. the desire to "leap" foreward from that spark.

Meditation: In this Name, in the sequence of the 72 Names of G-d; the previous name was an anxiety remedy that required an almost hypnotic remedy. Now this Name can come into force to re-animate the action of moving with alacrity. Like an athelete needs to calm their inner space, to be ready to spring/leap foreward coming from a composed mind/body/soul. This is a tool for a renewed alertness generated by the shining countenance of our Creator as opposed to reactive actions that have a genesis from a chaotic state. The "Countenance of G-d", which in Biblical terms, is G-d's attributes of Mercy and Tolerance, being the driving force of moving on. These attributes are also qualities we can utilize in our interaction with others.

The negative side of this angel dominates hate and hypocrisy; he rules those who seek to deceive by any possible means and keeps enemies irreconcilable.

MAY 5 – MAY 9
10th NAME OF G-D
IYAR 25 TO IYAR 29/SIVAN 1
LUNAR SIGN TAURUS/GEMINI

א ל ד

ALEPH LAMED DALET
A L D
1 + 30 + 4 = Gematria of 8

The God of Motion

Angel Intelligence: Eldaah

Root words:

אֶלְדָּעָה 'Elda`ah Eldaah

Notes Strongs #420: Proper Name Masculine;

from אל ['el] and יָדַע [yada`]; God of
knowledge;
Meaning: Eldaah = "God has known"
1) a son or descendant of Midian
AV translations: Eldaah.

אֵל 'el near, with, among, to

Notes Strongs #413: Preposition;
(but only used in the shortened constructive
form אֶל ['el]); a primitive particle; properly,
denoting motion towards, but occasionally used
of a quiescent position, i.e.
Meaning: 1) to, toward, unto (of motion)
2) into (limit is actually entered)
2a) in among
3) toward (of direction, not necessarily physical
motion)
4) against (motion or direction of a hostile
character)
5) in addition to, to

 6) concerning, in regard to, in reference to, on account of
 7) according to (rule or standard)
 8) at, by, against (of one's presence)
 9) in between, in within, to within, unto (idea of motion to)

יָלַד yalad to bear young, to beget, medically, to act as midwife, to show lineage

 Notes Strongs #3205: Verb;
 a primitive root;
 Meaning: 1) to bear, bringforth, beget, gender, travail
 1a) (Qal)
 1a1) to bear, bring forth
 1a1a) of child birth
 1a1b) of distress (simile)
 1a1c) of wicked (behaviour)
 1a2) to beget
 1b) (Niphal) to be born
 1c) (Piel)

1c1) to cause or help to bring forth
1c2) to assist or tend as a midwife
1c3) midwife (participle)
1d) (Pual) to be born
1e) (Hiphil)
1e1) to beget (a child)
1e2) to bear (fig. -of wicked bringing forth iniquity)
1f) (Hophal) day of birth, birthday (infinitive)
1g) (Hithpael) to declare one's birth (pedigree)
AV translations: bear, beget, birth(-day), born, (make to) bring forth (children, young), bring up, calve, child, come, be delivered (of a child), time of delivery, gender, hatch, labour, (do the office of a) midwife, declare pedigrees, be the son of, (woman in, woman that) travail(-eth, -ing woman).

Attributes/Function:
This Names bears the action of Knowledge. The D or Dalet is a function of Daat which is Knowing as well as D or Dalet is the symbol for a door. A door conceals, when it is opened, what is concealed is revealed, i.e. "known". Specifically

knowing inherently this thing is G-d, and the
opening of the door is granted by G-d. The other
root word of putting into motion, moving, or
"birthing" adds the aspect of understanding our
foreward motion is directed by G-d, this new or
added understanding of the aspect of G-d is
almost being re-born.

Aladiah: "The Angel of Secrets"

Type: Cherubim
Meaning: The Favorable God
Hebraic Translation: Alef Lamed Dalet Yod Hei

Attributes: Aladiah is good for those guilty of
hidden crimes, helps hide that which one does not
wish to reveal and fears discovery. Aladiah is a
protective shield.

This angel rules against rabies and plague, and
influences recovery from illnesses. The person who
is born under this influence enjoys good health, and
will be happy in his ventures/enterprises and highly
regarded by those who know him. He will frequent
the most sophisticated societies.

This Angel is associated with "Evil Eye" protection; not only those who are envious of you, but also your envious "looks" at others.

The negative side of this angel influences those who neglect their health and business.

MAY 10 – MAY 14
11th Name of G-d
Sivan 1 to Sivan 6
Lunar Sign of Gemini

לָאוּ

לָאֵל La'el Lael

 Notes Strongs #3815: Proper Name Masculine;
 from the prepositional prefix and אֵל ['el];
(belonging) to God;
 Meaning: Lael = "belonging to God"
 1) a Levite, father of Eliasaph and descendant of
Gershon
 AV translations: Lael.

Root word

אוּריאל 'Uwriy'el Uriel

Notes Strongs #222: Proper Name Masculine;
from אוּר ['uwr] and אל ['el]; flame of God;
Meaning: Uriel = "God (El) is my light"
1) chief of the Levitical line of Kohath in David's time
2) maternal grandfather of Abijah
AV translations: Uriel.

אוּאל 'Uw'el Uel

Notes Strongs #177: Proper Name Masculine;
from או ['ow] and אל ['el]; wish of God;
Meaning: Uel = "wish or will of God"

Attributes/Function:

The root words in this Name allude to "light of G-d; Wish of G-d, belonging to G-d. The previous name we are recipients of the G-d of Knowledge. Now we are the Lights of G-d, belonging to G-d, as the Creator desires us. We may wonder why we are here, with this Name, we put into effect by G-d wish and desire. What more justification do we need, from anyone. This is a strong spiritual connection to G-d as the One and Primary entity who created you/us as a desire to fulfill the Creator's and our mission here. The context of parents, siblings, friends in our lives is strong, and blessed are you when people in your life are supportive, however if they are not and are more toxic then healing, the One True Sanctuary is the Almighty in moving foreward, past any pain, any fear; or successes in the impermanent world.

Lauviah: "The Victe ory Angel"

Type: Cherubim
Meaning: The Exalted or Praised God

Attributes: Lauviah governs the obtainment of victory. He presides over the renowned, those of great personage, public figures, the learned and wise, and celebrities known for special talents.

He also protects against lightning, and cleanses your environment.

The negative side of this angel rules pride, ambition, jealousy and slander.

MAY 15 – MAY 19

12.   Hahaiah: "The Angel of Refuge"

Type: Cherubim
Meaning: God the Refuge

Attributes: Hahaiah guards against adversity, governs dreams and the mysteries hidden from mortals. He also rules over depths of despair, and reveals hidden mysteries to mortals. He influences wise, spiritual and discreet persons.

A person born under this influence has genial habits, witty, gentle, a pleasant physiognomy and agreeable manners.

The negative side of this angel rules indiscretion and untruth; he rules over all those who abuse peoples' trust.

MAY 20 – MAY 24

13. **Iezalel: "The Angel of Friendship"**

Type: Cherubim
Meaning: The God Sung/Glorified Above All

Attributes: Iezalel governs friendship, aids reconciliation, conjugal fidelity and dominates friendship. The attributes of this Angel are the ability to learn easily. A person born under this influence will learn everything he desires with ease; he will have happy memories and will distinguish himself through verbal communication. He will be sociable and have influence on memory and shrewdness.

This Angel is associated with the messiah as in experiencing divine purpose in ourselves and other. We realise the concept of heaven on earth.

The negative side of this angel rules over ignorance, error and lies, and influences limited souls who wish neither to learn nor to do anything.

MAY 25 – MAY 29

14th. Mebahel: "The Redemption Angel"

Type: Cherubim
Meaning: God the Protector and Savior, the Conservative God

Attributes: Mebahel aids against those who seek to usurp the fortunes of others. This Angel governs justice, truth, liberty. Mebahel delivers the oppressed and protects prisoners; loves jurisprudence, and has an affinity for law courts.

The Angel makes truth to be known and brings peaceful ends to conflicts.

The negative side of this angel rules over defamation and false actions.

MAY 30 – JUNE 3

15th Hariel

Type: Cherubim: "The Angel of Calm"
Meaning: The Comforting God

Attributes: Hariel governs sciences and arts, spiritual sentiments, and the ethically pure. One invokes this angel guards against the irreverent and the faithless. This angel influences useful discoveries and new methodologies.

The person born under this influence will be tuned into all things spiritual, sacred and tranquil; and also distinguish themselves through the purity and conviction of their principles.

The negative side of this angel rules over schisms, and religious wars; he influences the impious and all those who spread dangerous sects and seeks to re-establish them.

JUNE 4 TO JUNE 8

16th Hakamiah: "The Angel of War"

CHANGE ANGEL NUMBER 16

הקם

Mem Kof Hei
Water + Miracles/Boomerang quality of Soul +
Window/Breath of Life
"The breath of life from G-d to rebound, for divine
miracles, "water" is associated with the
Torah/Bible. In essence the Words of G-d, study of
Torah will intensify this "action".
400 + 100 + 5 = 505 = 10;1 Gematria number (also
"505" is gematrical number for Sarah)

Type: Cherubim
Meaning: The Rousing or Raising God

Attributes: Hakamiah warns of treason influences
fire, arsenals and all things connected with the
paraphernalia of war. He is the Angel of endurance
when the path appears unsurmountable. Hakamiah
is the Angel of strength to rise after a fall. He

guards against traitors and for deliverance from those who seek to oppress us. Hakamiah governs crowned heads, great captains and gives victory.

The person born under this Angel will be candid, loyal, brave, and sensitive to points of honor. This person has an affinity for Venus/Love and is faithful to his obligations.

The negative side of this angel rules over traitors; he provokes treason, troublemaking and revolt.

JUNE 9 TO JUNE 13

17th Lauviah: "The Endurance Angel"

Type: Thrones
Meaning: The Marvelous or Admirable God
Hebraic Translation: Lamed Alef Vav Yod Hei

Attributes: Lauviah is to be invoked while fasting. He guards against mental anguish and sadness. He gives revelations in dreams and the ability to sleep well at night. Lauviah governs high sciences and marvelous discoveries. The person born under this Angel loves music, poetry, literature and philosophy.

This Angel is associated with freedom from self-centeredness which is the greates cause of mental anguish. The "self" is replaced with family, friendship and achievement.

The negative side of this angel dominates non-belief and all those who attack spiritual systems of belief.

JUNE 14 TO JUNE 19

18th Caliel: "The Angel of Abundance/ Rapid Aid"

Type: Thrones
Meaning: The Invokable G-d
Hebraic Translation: Kaf Lamed Yod Aleph Lamed

Attributes: Caliel is the Angel to call to obtain prompt aid. This angel allows knowledge of truth in proceedings, lawsuits, and allows innocence triumph; he defeats the guilty and false testimony. Caliel dominates trials and influences witnesses. The person born under this influence will be just and possess integrity, love truth, and will distinguish himself in magistracy.

Meditation on this Angel is associated with abundance and fruitfulness. You will be imbued with the power of procreation. Your personal meditation is more powerful if you can also meditate upon others who are trying to start a family.

The Wrath/Retribution/Vengeance of this angel rules over scandalous processes, and influences vile, base and rampant men, and those who use unethical business practice to enrich themselves at the expense of their clients.

JUNE 20 TO JUNE 24

לֵוּו

19ᵗʰ Name of G-d: Lamed Vav Vav
LVV (letters read from right to left
30 + 6 + 6= Gematria of 6

Angel DerivationLeuviah

Type: Thrones
Attributes: This Name of G-d is a hypertext that
makes a direct connection to G-d. The root words
embedded here are a combination of uniting, joining
and cleaving with G-d and nailing or "hooking" to
the power that is The Almighty.
Meditation: This Name is saying/praying to G-d for
a direct connection; for purposes of guidance (if you
do or don't know exactly how to walk your path).
G-d supernally is attached to you and that joining to
G-d as a partner in life will carry us through the
most challenging times. In addition, even when our
lives are progressing extremely well, this Name also
unites us with our G-dly mission. Often in very
good times we may forget our purpose, or lose our

humility, so here in this Name we "continue to dance with The One that brought us" who is The Master of the Universe.

Root word: לֹו

לָוָה	*lavah*	to twine, to unite, to remain, to borrow, to lend
Notes		Strongs #3867: Verb; a primitive root;
Meaning:		1) to join, be joined 1a) (Qal) to join, be joined, attend 1b) (Niphal) to join oneself to, be joined unto 2) to borrow, lend 2a) (Qal) to borrow 2b) (Hiphil) to cause to borrow, lend to

Root Word:
וָו vav a hook

Notes Strongs #2053: Noun Masculine; probably
Meaning: 1) hook, peg, nail, pin

AV translations: hook.
Meaning: The swiftly harkening or listening God
Hebraic Translationa: Lamed Vav Vav Yod Hei

Leuviah is to be invoked while facing South. He
obtains the grace of God. This Angel governs
memory, human intelligence. One born under this
Angel will be amiable, lively, modest, bearing of
adversity with resignation. His attribute is the God
Who Forgives Sinners.

Meditation on this name can activate a direct
connection to God. You take in the name you dial,
you connect, and your truest prayers will be
answered at the speed of "Light". He protects and
aids in obtaining grace; dominates the memory,
influences joviality and intelligence.

JUNE 25 TO JUNE 30

20th Pahaliah

Type: Thrones
Hebraic Translation: Pey Hei Lamed Yod Hei

Attributes: God the Redeemer

Pahaliah – This Angel governs against enemies of religion, theology, morality, chastity, purity. His attribute is Redemptor God. He influences chastity and piety in those whose vocation is towards the ecclesiastical state.

Meditation on this Angel will make you ready to battle the nasty habits and unpleasant character traits that you have not been able to get rid of. This Name ensures victory over the forces of ego. It will imbue you with the emotional power and discipline to triumph over all self-centered impulses and negative desires.

The negative side of this angel rules irreligion, deserter, absconder, libertines and betrayer.

JULY 1 TO JULY 5

21. Nelchael: "The Magic Charm Angel"

נָהַל nahal to run with a, sparkle, flow, to conduct, to protect, sustain

Notes Strongs #5095: Verb;
a primitive root;
Meaning: 1) to lead, give rest, lead with care, guide to a watering place or station, cause to rest, bring to a station or place of rest, guide, refresh
1a) (Piel)
1a1) to lead to a watering-place or station and cause to rest there
1a2) to lead or bring to a station or goal
1a3) to lead, guide
1a4) to give rest to
1a5) to refresh (with food)
1b) (Hithpael)
1b1) to lead on

1b2) to journey by stations or stages
AV translations: carry, feed, guide, lead (gently, on).
from יָלַךְ [yalak]; a journey;

Type: Thrones
Attributes: The Only God

Nelchael aids in *magic* charms and for the destruction of evil spirits and *plagues* by summoning forth Light. This Angel also rules over astronomy, mathematics, geography and all abstract sciences. The person born under this influence loves poetry, literature, avid for study and will distinguish themselves in mathematics and geometry. His attribute is the aspect of God as One and Unique.

The negative side of this angel rules ignorance, error and prejudice.

JULY 6 TO JULY 10
22nd Name of God
YOD YOD YOD
10+10+10=Gematria of 3

יּיּיּ

YYY

Attributes: This Name is the manifestation of enlightenment. Yod is direction and purpose, it is the Omnipresence revealed, the hand of G-d guiding, thrusting you forward and the wave nature of radiation, e.g. light: The triplicate of this Yod is significant as a cubed number. This is a blast of perfect light, no chaser.

Meditation:

Enlightening our world, the existential revelation of G-d's hand and light moving us forward. And the property of the Light, banishes harmful forces in all it's forms from our presence.

יָאִיר Ya'iyr Jair

Notes Strongs #2971: Proper Name Masculine; from אוֹר ['owr]; enlightener; Meaning: Jair = "he enlightens"

1) a descendant of Manasseh who conquered
many towns during the time of the conquest
 2) the Gileadite, a judge of Israel for 22 years
during the time of the judges; father of 30 sons
 3) a Benjamite, son of Kush, and father of
Mordecai
 4) father of Elhanan, one of David's mighty
warriors
 AV translations: Jair.

JULY 11 TO JULY 15

23.   Melahel: "The Angel that Banishes Evil"

Type: Thrones
Meaning: The God Deflecting Evil

Attributes: Melahel guards against weapons and for
safety in travel. He governs water, produce of the
earth, and especially plants necessary to cure
disease.

The person born under this influence is naturally
resilient and capable of undertaking the most
dangerous expeditions.

The negative side of this angel influences all that is harmful to vegetation; he causes illnesses and plague.

JULY 16 TO JULY 20

24. Hahuiah: "The Angel of Grace"
Type: Thrones
Meaning: God of Mercy and Consternation

Attributes : Hahuiah serves to obtain grace and mercy from God. This angel rules over refugees, exiles and condemned prisoners; he works to aid against the discovery of a person's secret crimes, and those people who commit them will escape justice provided they do not fall back into the same criminal ways. He protects against dangerous creatures, robbers and assassins.

Hahuiah's influence is the love of truth, sincerity and exact sciences.

The negative side of this angel rules over harmful beings; he leads men to commit crimes, and influences all those who seek to live by unlawful means.

JULY 21 TO JULY 25

25. Nith-haiah: "The Angel of Secrets"

Type: Dominions
Hebraic Translation: Nun Tet Hei Hei Yod
Attributes: The Generous God

The Angel Nith-Haiah serves to gain wisdom and to discover the truth of hidden secrets. This angel rules over all the mystical/esoteric/sciences, ability to detect hidden processes or phenomena by observing manifest unexplained phenomena (for example pinpointing a hidden medical event that results in an observable peripheral event using diagnostics/analytics); he gives revelations in dreams; particularly to those born on the day over which he rules. Nith-haiah influences wise men who love peace, seek truth and solitude; and those who practice the magic of the sages, which is that of God.

This Angel compels you to tell the truth and to hear it.

The negative side of this angel rules over black magic and those who renounce the Light. He brings malevolence to mankind, animals and to products of the earth.

JULY 26 TO JULY 31

26. Haaiah: "The Angel of Law"

Type: Dominons
Attributes: God Listening in Concealment

The Angel Haaiah aids in winning of law suits. He serves to win judgments and to render judges favorable. This angel protects all those who seek the truth; he brings men to the contemplation of divine things; he rules over politicians, diplomats, plenipotentiaries, ambassadors, peace treaties, dealings and all pacts in general; he influences couriers, communications, agents and secret expeditions.

This Angel says harmony always underlies chaos; Order emerges from chaos. Your capacity to land on your feet is restored

The negative side of this angel rules over traitors, the ambitious and conspirators.

AUGUST 1 TO AUGUST 5

27. Jerathel: "The Angel of Prevention"

Type: Dominions
Attributes: The Preventing God

The Angel Jerathel aids in confusing wrong-doers and liars and protects those who provoke and unjustly attack us. Jerathel delivers us from our enemies; he governs propagation of light, civilization, peace, justice, science and arts.

Jerathel's attribute is the God who punishes the Wicked.

The negative side of this angel rules over ignorance, slavery and intolerance.

AUGUST 6 TO AUGUST 10

28. Seheiah: "The Angel of Longevity"

Type: Dominions
Attributes: God Who Heals the Ill

Seheiah governs health, simplicity and longevity of life. This Angel guards against frailty, thunder, fire, the ruin of buildings, falls and illnesses. The person born under this influence will have good judgment and act with prudence and alertness.

This Angel is associated with soul mate energy.

The negative side of this angel rules over catastrophes, accidents and the cause of apoplexies; he influences people who don't think before acting.

AUGUST 11 TO AUGUST 15

29. Reiiel: "The Angel of Deliverance"

Type: Dominions
Attributes: The God Quick to Help

Reiiel governs the deliverance from all enemies both visible and invisible. Reiiel attributes are virtue and zeal for the dissemination of truth and will do his utmost to destroy negative feelings and personal transgressions through literature and by example.

The negative side of this angel rules over fanaticism and hypocrisy; he rules over all those who propagate irreverence through writings and dangerous maxims.

AUGUST 16 TO AUGUST 20

30. Omael: "The Angel of Patience"

Type: Dominions
Attributes: The Patient God

Omael guards against sorrow, despair and for the acquisition of patience. He governs animal kingdom, watches over the procreation and evolution of beings in order to see the generations of men and animals multiply and races perpetuated. He influences chemists, doctors and surgeons. The person born under this influences will distinguish himself in anatomy and medicine.

This Angel influences conflict resolutions and finds the way forward to initiate those contacts.

The negative side of this angel is the enemy of propagation of beings; he influences monstrous phenomena.

AUGUST 21 TO AUGUST 25

31. Lecabel: "The Achievement Angel"

Type: Dominions
Meaning: God the Teacher

Attributes:

Lecabel aids to finish what you start; to conclude everything you begin, especially tasks and goals of spiritual nature. He governs the acquisition of knowledge, vegetation and agriculture. The person born under this influence will love astronomy, mathematics and geometry. They will distinguish themselves through brilliant ideas and resolving the most difficult problems.

The negative side of this angel rules over greed and usury. He influences those who enrich themselves by illicit means.

AUGUST 26 TO AUGUST 31

32. Vasariah: "The Angel of Justice"

Type: Dominions
Meaning: The Good God, or: The Just God

Attributes:

Vasariah is the Angel that fights against those who attack us in courts. He governs justice, good memory, and being articulate. The invocation of this Angel aids to obtain the grace of those who have recourse to obtain the forgiveness by authority. This angel rules over justice, influences nobility, legal executives, magistrates and attorneys.

The person born under this influence will have a good memory and speak eloquently with ease. Vasariah has the quality of this to influence the cosmos with words.

The negative side of this angel rules over all the negative qualities of the body and the soul.

SEPTEMBER 1 TO SEPTEMBER 5

33. Iehuiah

Meaning: God Who Knows All Things or: The omniscient God
Type: Virtue
Hebraic Translation: Yod Hei Vav Yod Hei

Attributes:

Iehuiah aids in revealing the dark side to help you to recognize the negetive forces still active inside you. This Angel aids to over come your dark side, your negetive impulses; and for the identification of traitors to destroy their projects and their machinations. This angel protects all spiritual princes; he keeps their subjects in obeisance. The person born under this influence will love to fulfill all the works of his estate (state).

Meditate on this Angel make the Light shines and recognize the negative forces still active within you.

They are no longer a mystery and they become
history!

The person who was born under this influence will
enables us to integrate God and Spiritual Energy, by
integrating the energy of the Son, as if we became
God. We then serve this interior god with love and
devotion, by respect of the Light and the divinity
which is of each one of us, and who touches any
incarnée life.

Angel Iehuiah says to us that our vocation is to
serve God, to serve each one among us, to be
conscious of the place which we occupy in the
Universe and of the precise role that we have to
play. It gives a great energy of faith and bravery
enabling us to act by glorifiant God and His work.
It brings the power of the action and construction to
raise each one of us towards a better life,
overwhelmed love and of compassion. It knows that
any place has its importance in the Plan of Creation
and that any change can occur but only if each one
knows its duty, its work and that it achieves it with
accuracy and justice.

The negative side of this angel rules over insubordinate beings; he provokes the seditious to revolt.

SEPTEMBER 6 TO SEPTEMBER 10

34. Lehahiah

Meaning: The Gentle God
God Clement
Type: Virtue
Hebraic Translation: Lamed Hei Chet Hei Yod Hei

Attributes:

Lehahiah's attribute is the Gentle God. This angel
rules over crowned heads, princes and nobles; he
maintains harmony, understanding and peace
between them; He useful against anger; he
influences the obedience of subjects towards their
princes. The person born under this influence will
become famous through his talents and his actions;
he will have the confidence and favor of his prince,
which he will merit because of his devotion,
trustworthiness and the great service which he will
render him.

By meditating on this name you will transcend the
limits of your own being. It will cling to the Tree of

Life. Happiness will find you, now that your ego is out of the spotlight. You can get out of your own way, letting go of all stubbornness.

Angel Lehahiah helps the people completing an important work for Humanity. They have an essential place in the advance of Humanity today and allow an awakening of conscience so that the Era of Aquarius is set up. These people work is within the framework of a group, a community, of a company, but always in a regrouping of individuals. They feel called, practically obliged to occupy themselves of the others, to open ways, doors to them, and possibilities of leaving their imprisonment (physical, moral or mental). These beings have in fact a collective karma with these groups and their mission consists in raising the hearts towards the release and the take-off to be, by allowing the return to them towards the Light.

Angel Lehahiah is the incarnate of peace, brings the peace of the heart which so often took the wrong way. It is there to explain why peace and forgiveness were always present, but that we did not want to hear it because we censure ourselves.

Forgiveness always was there because the Light of God always transmutes the events and the actions which were not right. It is enough for us simply, in our turn, to transmute these actions by the flame of Love and Light which lives us. Transmute

Angel Lehahiah infuses us with the gift of perseverance and patience so that we can achieve the task which consists in accompanying each one in the achievement by its life. It also enables us to prevent that we turn over in our old operations. The Law which Angel Lehahiah transmits is a law of purification by the service. Angel LEHAHIAH shows us that we are not there to rebuild systems which are clean for us, but simply altering the existing systems.

The negative side of this angel rules over discord; he provokes war, treason and the ruin of nations.

SEPTEMBER 11 TO SEPTEMBER 15

35. Chavakiah

Meaning: God Who Gives the Joy
Type: Virtue
Hebraic Translation: Kaf Vav Quoph Yod Hei

Attributes:

Chavakiah aids to regain the favor of those one has
offended. He Governs testaments, successions and
all private financial agreements. Loves to live in
peace with everyone. Loves rewarding the loyalty
of those in his service and all amiable distributions;
he supports peace and harmony in families. The
person born under this influence will love
living in peace with everybody, even to the cost of
his interest; he will make it his duty to repay the
fidelity and good offices of those in his service.

Meditation with this Angel purify desires, bring you
to share love and energy with partners, putting his
or her needs ahead of your own. You ignite sexual
energy so that your passion helps elevate all

existence. You replenish the Light that was lost due to any prior selfish sexual activities.

The Light can be set up only if we agree to look in us our basic structures, comprising our qualities but also our defects, in order to rebalance them. The Light settles then in a stability which we really build and internalize. The least interior destabilization weakens the force of this Light. Angel Chavakiah helps us to find this balance and shows us, permanently; where we are in the error, in order to reinstall this Light and connection with the Divine one.

Angel Chavakiah is carrying a great energy of reconciliation with ourselves. It encourages us to reconcile us with all the external people with whom we are in conflict. It leads this energy in order to spread a new energy of peace in the world. This aspiration with peace comes from a memory related to Atlantis, which at the present time follows and touches practically all Humanity."

The negative side of this angel causes discord in family arrangements; he provokes unjust and ruinous procedures.

SEPTEMBER 16 TO SEPTEMBER 20

36. Menadel

Meaning: The Adorable God
Type: Virtue
Hebraic Translation: Mem Nun Dalet Aleph Lamed

Atttributes:

Menadel serves to retain one's employment and to preserve one's means of livelihood which one enjoys. He serves against calamities and to deliver prisoners. This angel gives light to distant people who have received no news for a long time; he brings exiles back to their native land, and uncovers mislaid or disturbed belongings.

Meditate on this Name bring courage to conquer fears rising within you . By proactively confronting your fears at the seed level, you will yank them out by the roots and remove them entirely from your being.

Angel Menadel represents the power of the love. It
is the Fire of heaven which is transferred only by
the gift of ourselves and the love which we
succeeded in integrating. This is not done without
certain difficulties, and Angel Menadel helps us by
his great softness, its support and its gift of service.
It helps us to separate us from our past and of all
that attaches us and prevents us from advancing in
the Light and the Love.

Angel Menadel says to us, do not remain not
centered on yourselves and act. Act with accuracy
and heart. Work can be different for each one, but
any work has its importance and it is necessary to
believe in this importance to include/understand
your place in the Universe. Work is a key of our
existence and Angel Menadel enables us to like
work, and to include/understand the hidden
direction of it. Because any work, whatever it is, has
a raison d'être, which is not always that which is
visible at first sight. This work can prepare us with
other things, or make us work towards
perseverance, endurance, patience, or prepare us
with a future work. It can sometimes to also open us

in certain state of consciousnesses, or new
responsibilities, or new interior transformations.

So then, let us accept any work like a gift of the sky,
and not like an obligation. Work brings an energy
which represents the continuation of the Life, so
that this one can provide food, support the family
and of course, of the power of the love which wakes
up the richness inside of each one of us.

*The negative side of this angel rules protects all
those who seek to flee abroad to escape justice.*

SEPTEMBER 21 TO SEPTEMBER 25

37. Aniel: "The Angel of Victory"

Meaning: God Lord of all virtues
Heirarchy Rank: Virtue Angel
Hebraic Translation: Alef Nun Yod Alef Lamed

Attributes:

Aniel's attribute is God of Virtues who serves to
obtain victory and stop the siege of a city
(civilization). This angel rules over the sciences
and the arts; he reveals the secrets of nature and
inspires wise philosophers with their meditations.
The person born under this influence will acquire
celebrity through his talents and his enlightenment,
and he will distinguish himself among the wise.

Meditation upon this Angel e raises awareness of
the long-term effects of your own actions. You can
gain the ability to see the spiritual challenges in
every moment, before they become the foundations
of chaos and crises.

Angel Aniel helps us to gain the victory over
ourselves, and to renew our life in order to continue
it in the Light, clearness, the communion and the
good agreement with the others. He says to us that
the Light is in us, that we know it well, that we will
work it for a long time. The Light is balance and our
current role consists to radiate it and propagate it
around us.

Angel Aniel confers the energy of a leader who acts
to build and balance and which offers to the world
its service and duty towards the spiritual planes. It
explains us a new approach of the spiritual plane,
whose fuel has been the same since all eternity but
needs to be opened with other realities, according to
the evolution of Humanity. The Angel Aniel brings
light and discoveries to new concepts in this matter
of evolution. It inspires us to discover advances in
the Human condition in the discovery, cure,
creation and care of Life, care of the Life to achieve
equilibrium with Divine Law.

*The negative side of this angel rules over perverse
spirits; he influences charlatans and all those who
excel in the art of misleading men.*

SEPTEMBER 26 TO SEPTEMBER 30

38. Haamiah

Meaning: God The Hope of All the Creatures on
The Earth
Type: Virtue
Hebraic Translation: Chet Ayin Mem Yod Hei

Attributes:

Haamiah's attribute is God, the Hope of All the
Children of the Earth . One calls upon these divine
names to acquire all the treasures of the Sky and the
Earth. He works against thunder, arms, ferocious
beasts and infernal spirits. This angel rules over all
religious worship, and above all those which relate
to God; it protects all those which seek truth.

Meditation on this Name helps to receive when you
share and to share when you receive. You can see
the opportunity that sharing gives and will make
you aware that when you receive with the right
consciousness, you also share. This is the wire of
life you move from darkness to the Light.

Angel Haamiah invites each one among us to discover his own spiritual search and to restore the contact between God and the men. For that, it shows us where our force is. It enables us to be the Carrier of Light which becomes pillar of Light, transmitter of Light. It channels simply at the energy level where the Light is retransmitted with planet. This mechanism, by effect of the Law of Resonance, makes it possible to bring peace in the Universe.

Angel Haamiah brings the energy of guidance, the possibilityof being guided but also to guide others. This Angel gives the man his function first which is to be the initiator of the Earth and the Universe. To carry out this mission we must find this role in our living from and our role of mediator between the Earth and the Sky.

Angel Haamiah carries Humankind towards his higher aspirations to adore the Life again and to find this conscience of the alliance of Life to Love, one not existing without the other.

The Wrath/Retribution Power of this angel rules over error and falsehood and influences all those who have no religious principles.

OCTOBER 1 TO OCTOBER 5

39. Rehael

Meaning: God Who Receives the Sinners
Type: Virtue
Hebraic Translation: Reish Hei Ayin Aleph Lamed

Attributes:

Rehael is the quickly forgiving God. This Angel recognizes the diamond in the rough, helping transform negative situations into positive opportunities and blessings. He helps to bring into your life what your soul desires.

Rehael governs the healing of the sick; health and longevity. He influences paternal and parental affection the obedience and respect of children for their parents.

By meditating on this Angel you accomplish nothing less than the complete transformation of negative situations into positive opportunities and blessings. Life begins to manifest anything your soul desires or imagines.

Angel Rehael is the Light which lights the way of the Knowledge of the Life. It teaches us to detect any internal imbalance and to cure it by acquired knowledge, data or which comes from outside. It also learns how to us to detect any external agent which can bring us imbalance and step aside from it. It helps us to meet the good people, be in the places of a favorable life with our evolution and the personal work we need.

Angel Rehael also gives us the knowledge we need to be the vehicle to cure and cure ourselves. Tools of Light appear to facilitate cures. This Angel gives a new point of view on the concept of freedom, because freedom does not mean to attack the freedom of the others, but to live in real harmony with each one and each thing, so that all has its right place without having to encroach on the space of the other to live or breathe. The concept of freedom is the release of the ego in relation to itself. When this is created no holds barred freedom can start to be set up.

The negative side of this angel is called Terre Morte or Terre Damnee following the expression of Eteilla, in his Philosophy of High Sciences, He is the most cruel and treacherous of all; he influences infanticides and parricides.

OCTOBER 6 TO OCTOBER 10

40. Ieiazel

Meaning: God Who Delights
Type: Virtue
Hebraic Translation: Yod Yod Zayin Aleph Lamed

Attributes:

Ieiazel aids in the deliverance of prisoners, for consolation, for deliverance from one's enemies. This angel rules over printing and libraries and books; he influences men of letters and artists. The person born under this influence will love speaking, reading, drawing, design, and all sciences in general.

Meditate on this Angel to silence your ego. Call upon the Light to speak on for you in all situations, so that your every word elevates your soul and all existence.

Angel Ieiazel gets us in contact with our acquired wisdom. It says to us that our interior fire and instincts are controlled. This is to keep them under control and balance our harmony in order to avoid their reappearance which gives us useless duality. New tests are given each day in order to show us where our Light is and the lessons which we learned. This process enables us to go further in the realization that Life is not static, it is perpetual change, training. Our wisdom was given to us by God.

Angel Ieiazel reminds us that God gave us the Life via two complementary energies, the masculine and the female one, thanks to the balance of these two energies. It pushes us to materialize this balance in our life every day to carry out this state of harmony in all that we create. Angel Ieiazel gives us the joy of acting and the joy of answering the wills of the Heavens.

Ieiazel is paramountly associated with water which gives Life. Life, which grows thanks to heat of the Sun and the Fire of the Earth. Life is based on the union of the force of the masculine and female, of the sun and water, the man and the woman. This Angel makes us the conscience of the Life which we carry in us and of the care that we owe it. This is the extremely important foundation that each one of us carries, man or woman, all Co-creators of God.

The negative side of this angel rules over all evil qualities of the body and soul; he influences somber spirits and those who flee society.

OCTOBER 11 TO OCTOBER 15

41. Hahahel

Meaning: God in Three People
Type: Power
Hebraic Translation: Hei Hei Hei Aleph Lamed

Attributes:

Hahahel aids against the impious, slanderers.
Governs Christianity. Greatness of soul, energy.
Consecrated to the service of God.   His attribute is
God in Three Persons.

This Angel is useful against the enemies of the
religion, the irreligious people and the slanderers.
This Genius dominates over Christianity; it protects
the missionaries and all the disciples from Christ,
who announce the words of the Gospel to the
nations; it influences the pious hearts, the prelates,
the ecclesiastics, and all that is referred to
priesthood.

The person who was born under this influence will distinguish by her nobility of soul and her energy; she will devote herself entirely to the service of God, and she will not fear to suffer the martyr for Christ.

The person born under this influence distinguishes himself by his greatness of soul and his energy; he is completely devoted to the service of God and does not fear martyrdom for Christ.

By meditating with this Angel you are connected to the power of the ancient high priests of the temple to heal all areas of life including health problems, financial difficulties, and relationship conflicts.

Angel Hahahel says to us that we are with the state of study and that our affiliation with God is real and large. This force makes us grow and gives us major joy. This joy needs to be expressed with humanity. The more we feel the happiness of humankind, the more intense our joy is.

Angel Hahahel leads us to influence others, to try to bring to them the same state of happiness and bliss.

The Light which shines through us is not always understood, but we are capable to persevere in our step because we know that we will always touch somebody at a given time.

There are fundamental Laws to discover, and God shows us in three people, ourselves, the female and of the masculine; the Three, the final creative element is created can take its place in our conscience in this universe created by God.

The negative side of this angel rules over apostates, renegades and all those who dishonor the priesthood through their scandalous behavior

OCTOBER 16 TO OCTOBER 20

42. Michael

Meaning: House of God, similar to God
Type: Power
Hebraic Translations: Mem Yod Kaf Aleph Lamed

Attributes:

Michael reveals the concealed; the genuine light of the Creator and the ultimate truths of life are also first concealed and then revealed. It is up to us to uncover these truths to restore light into the world. He serves to travel in safety. This angel rules monarchs, princes and nobles; he keeps their subjects subservient, uncovers conspiracies and all those who seek to destroy their persons and governments. The person born under this influence will become involved in political affairs; he will be curious, and will want to learn the secrets of private offices and foreign news, and he will distinguish himself in affairs of State through his knowledge of diplomacy.

By meditate on this Angel to garner the ability to bring forth the powers of observation to see the truth . . . and the courage to handle it!

Thus, when cycle of a heart ends, doesn't it give birth to a new heart? Doesn't the cycle of a flower which dies make another flower blossom? Our responsibility with the life, is life itself. To learn how to like it, respect it, maintain it and follow its cycle renewed unceasingly and eternal. Our responsibility consists to accomodate it, to accept it and all will be simpler. This responsibility will become then a gift and either a burden.

Angel Michael shows us that we must assume these responsibilities and that they are not delegated. Each one has their own level which is their own. We receive the responsibilities that we are largely able to handle under the assumption we hold the capacity to do so.

Angel Michael puts us in contact with the intentions of the angelica plans and celestial. It traces us the road which we have to achieve. This participation in the plans of the Universe is always

done by a close cooperation with the others.
Michael is to some extent a guard, one of the pillars
of our building of Light and our body of Light.

*The negative side of this angel rules over traitors;
he influences malevolence and all those who
propagate false information.*

OCTOBER 21 TO OCTOBER 25

43. Veualiah

Meaning: God Who Dominates
Type: Power
Hebraic Translation: Vav Vav Lamed Yod Hei

Attributes:

Veualiah attriubutes are God, king and ruler. This angel rules over peace and influences the prosperity of empires; he affirms tottering thrones and kingly power. The person born under this influence will love the military state and glory; he will be continually engaged in those sciences which are in rapport with the angel of war; he will become famous through the means of arms, and will attract the confidence of his prince through the services he renders him. He is used to destroy the enemy and to be delivered from slavery.

Meditate on this Angel to unleash the power of mind over matter, soul over ego, and the spiritual over the physical. You can control your reality by the power of your mind. Everything becomes possible!

Angel Veualiah conveys Divine Energy in the form of Divine Justice, a Divine Justice when personified quite simply brings balance. This Angel brings the charisma to that which must be the right arm of God and who is intended to bring the Energy of God

The person carried by Angel Veualiah "dominates" the world by their internal power, the power of God. To dominate means here to serve a high vision, that of the Creator, who sees all and knows all and that remains humble and modest. Such is the richness of this person; peace becomes its objective, synonymous with serenity and plenitude. By this energy, we seek the source this serenity first and in kind create an atmosphere of peace and joy around us.

The negative side of this angel puts discord between princes; he influences the destruction of empires; he supports revolutions and party spirit.

OCTOBER 26 TO OCTOBER 30

44. Ielahiah

Meaning: God the Eternal and Lasting
Type: Powers
Hebraic Translation: Yod Lamed Hei Yod Hei

Attributes:

Ielahiah is invoked this to obtain success in a useful
enterprise; He is good for getting the protection of
magistrates and to win a lawsuit. This angel
protects against arms; he gives victory. The person
born under this influence will love to travel in order
to learn, and will succeed in all his undertakings; he
will distinguish himself through his military talents
and his bravery, and his name will be famous in the
display of glory.

Through meditation upon this sequence and with
genuine penitence in your heart, you can lessen or
even revoke judgments set forth against you.
Meditate to offer mercy and compassion to others.

With the Angel Ielahiah, any object, any act takes another value and Life is very different. It gives us desire for living it differently, with equity and accuracy. This moment in Life radiates Light and returns it to the Cosmos, which will be used in a future time, for other beings and other planets.

Angel Ielahiah helps us to express ourselves in our work, whatever it maybe, and to radiate this energy of Light, make it material and thus write our own daily history, of this Life, everyday so the meaning of Life becomes different. It is Love, light and understanding. Life is our guide and teacher.

The negative side of this angel rules over war, and causes all the calamities which arise from it; he influences all those who violate surrenders and massacre their prisoners without pity.

OCTOBER 31 TO NOVEMBER 4

45. Sealiah

Meaning: The God who Raises up all Men
Type: Power
Hebraic Translation: Samech Aleph Lamed Yod Hei

Attributes:

Sealiah has the Power of Prosperity. He serves to confound evil, authoritarianism, and the haughty; he lifts up all those who are humiliated and fallen. This angel rules over vegetation; he bears life and health for everything that breathes and influences the principal agents of Nature. The person born under this influence will love to learn and he will have many resources. This Angel helps to develop self identity, the capacity to be in control and develop humility, and fights against vanity.

By meditating on this Angel you acknowledge that the Light of the Creator is the supreme source of all prosperity. With this Angel you summon the forces of prosperity, well-being and sustenance. He assists is maintaining your humility when prosperity starts manifesting in abundance in your life.

The negative side of this angel rules over the atmosphere; he incites great heat or cold, great aridity or excessive humidity.

NOVEMBER 5 TO NOVEMBER 9

46. Ariel: "The Angel of Treasure and Revelation"

Meaning: The Revealing God
Type: Power
Hebraic Translation: Ayin Reish Yod Aleph Lamed

Attributes:

Ariel is the Angel who discovers ancient/hidden treasures; he reveals the greatest secrets of Nature and he shows the objects of one's desires in dreams. The person born under this influence is blessed with a strong and subtle spirit; he will have original ideas and sublime thoughts; he will be able to resolve the most difficult problems; he will be discreet and will act with much circumspection. One calls upon this Angel to have revelations; it is used to thank God for the good(s) that is sent to us.

The Angel Ariel clarifies the destiny of each one (as in people in general). Its evocative Light makes one discover all the beauties and kindness of this world. Ariel gives us clarity and the understanding for using these qualities for wellness, so that they cannot be used for personal ends. The love is an invaluable gift which we must give without differentiating among those who really need it versus those who use it to control others.   It is unconditional.

Angel Ariel says to us: "Learn how to listen to others with the heart and not the mental influence". Ariel understands there exists many in humanity, whom in the name of the love, handle other people according to their own suitability and personal imagination. However, Love is the greatest energy of Light which you receive. You are Love. Bless All on Earth with this love.

Angel Ariel always pushes us to flood humanity with love, but also to close the floodgates when the time comes. This Love for some is synonymous with seduction. This Love brings a certain charisma and a deep respect. The seduction forms part our egotistic being which prevents us from entering the Love fully. The being who fully captures the love being always develops God and his teaching; and this love is always beautiful and in unconditional. This Love always opens all the doors that are in union with Divine energy.

The Angel Ariel highlights that the application of the Laws of the Love around us is carried out in the Spirit and that the key of this Realization is there. The more we activate ourselves in the spiritual conscience, the more we are illuminated. Thus we are in real "synch" with our Life and the Universe can entrust its Secrets to us and open the doors to the subtle worlds of Universal Law.

The negative side of this angel causes tribulations of spirit; he brings men to commit the greatest indiscretions and influences feeble people.

NOVEMBER 10 TO NOVEMBER 14

47. Asaliah

Meaning: God the just Judge
Type: Power
Hebraic Translation: Ayin Shin Lamed Yod Hei

Attributes:

Asaliah's attribute is the Just God, Who Points To Truth . This angel rules over justice, men of honesty, and over those who raise their spirit to the contemplation of divine things. The person born under this influence will have an agreeable character; he will be passionate to acquire secret light.

Meditating on this Angel will bring you to understand the spiritual truth that world peace begins with peace in your own heart. Thus you can quickly develop your own transformation and strengthen the forces of peace throughout the world.

This Angel brings wisdom by a deep felt interior, the ability to feel what's in the hearts of humankind and thereby guessing their thoughts. He opens hearts which introduces the Divine Wisdom transmits from heart to heart the thoughts of wisdom and love.

The negative side of this angel rules over immoral and scandalous acts, and over all those who spread dangerous and chimerical schemes.

NOVEMBER 15 TO NOVEMBER 19

48. Mihael: "The Rescue Angel"

Meaning: God the Helpful Father
Type: Power

Attributes:

Mihael's attribute is God, the Rescuing Father. He serves to preserve peace and union between married couples. This angel protects those who have turned to him. They will have premonition and secret inspiration about all that will happen to them. He rules over the creation of humanity, influences friendship and conjugal fidelity. The person born under this influence will be passionate for love and all pleasure in general.

Angel Mihael helps all those which are in half-light and all the hearts which are lost or wandering, like those which are blocked between two worlds. He helps them to find the Light within them; drives out any fear and brings back confidence, peace and faith with tenderness and gentleness.

The energy of Angel Mihael also makes it possible to integrate and balance sexual energy. This makes it possible to generate life (procreate) as well as experience the totality of all different levels of love. Any person who has experienced love towards their father, mother, wife, husband, or child has total experience of this love and the ability to discover all its facets. You focus upon harmony and soul not selfish desires.

The negative side of this angel rules over luxury, sterility and fickleness and creates dissension, jealousy, and conflict between married.

NOVEMBER 20 TO NOVEMBER 24

49. Vehuel: "The Glory Angel"

Type: Principality
Meaning: Great and Exalted God

Attributes:

Vehuel serves to make one have intensity towards God, to bless Him and to glorify Him, when one is touched with admiration. This angel rules over great people and those who raise themselves and distinguish themselves through their talents and virtues. The person born under this influence will have a sensitive and generous nature; he will be held in esteem and will distinguish himself in literature, jurisprudence and diplomacy.

This Angel is associated with deep appreciaton for whatever life has in store for us which brings happiness.

The negative side of this angel rules over egotistical men; he rules hate and hypocrisy.

NOVEMBER 25 TO NOVEMBER 29

50. Daniel: "The Angel of Devotion, Mercy and Consolation"

Type: Principality
Meaning: God the Merciful Judge

Attributes:

Daniel aids to obtain the mercy of God and consolation. This angel rules over justice, counsels, attorneys and magistrates in general. He gives inspiration to those who are encumbered by many things, and don't know how to make decisions. The person born under this influence will be industrious and active in business; he will love literature and will distinguish himself through his eloquence. The Angel Daniel brings the balance of the Justice of God and the concept of equity.

This Angel is associated with focus to reach a goal and persistence.

The Angel Daniel conveys a concept of unlimited, timeless and immortal love. It regenerates the body and heart beyond the physical laws and contacts Divine Law.

The negative side of this angel rules over those who live by their wits, and all those who abhor work and who seek to live by illicit means.

DECEMBER 1 TO DECEMBER 4

51. Hahasiah: "The Angel of Secrets"

Meaning: God, the impenetrable Secret
Type: Principalities

Attributes:

Hahasiah rules over chemistry and physics; he reveals the greatest of Nature's secrets, notably the Philosopher's Stone and the Universal Physic. The person born under this influence will love abstract sciences; he will be particularly attracted to the knowledge of the properties and virtues attributed to animals, vegetables and minerals; he will be distinguished in medicine through wonderful cures, and he will make many discoveries useful to society.

This Angel is associated with spiritual repentence to repair past sins.

Angel Hahasiah brings intuition and an opening to the spiritual plane. When we arrive in contact with

God, we can start the process of cure of our physical body, since it is His representation on a denser level, we are all God's physical house.

The negative side of this angel rules over con artists and all those who abuse others' good faith, by promising them extraordinary things.

DECEMBER 5 TO DECEMBER 9

52. Imamiah: "The Angel of the Arts"

Type: Principalities
Meaning: High God Above All Things

Attributes:

Imamiah represents Spiritual art as it is intended to take its rightful place as formerly in our history. This art makes it possible to contact the Divine one. These images are channeled by the conscience of the painter and Beings of Light. Imamiah rules over all travel in general; he protects prisoners who call upon him; and inspires in them the way to obtain their liberty; he influences all those who seek the truth of good faith, and turn away from their mistakes by making a truly sincere return to God. The person born under this influence will have a strong and vigorous temperament; he will bear adversity with patience and courage; and will complete everything he wishes with ease.

Angel Imamiah gives courage to all those who are influenced by their heart to establish Life and to procreate. The Angel Imamiah represents the sublimation of the love, the transformation of the sexual instinct into a sublimated and shared worldly love. This mechanism bypasses sexuality and causes the integration of our two polarities, which particularly concentrates on the female polarity, which enables us to discover and trust our intuition. The Heart of the Mother and the heart of the world are identified with the Angel Imamiah.

The negative side of this angel rules over pride, blasphemy and evil; he influence boorish and quarrelsome men.

DECEMBER 10 TO DECEMBER 14

53. Nanael: "The Angel of Humility"

Type: Principalities
Meaning: God who Lowers the Proud Ones

Atttributes:

Angel Nanael shows us that it is love which controls our life and allows us to see the joy in life as opposed to self-interest, ulterior motives, and hidden agendas. Love shows the true face of the world and reflects the Light of God, the Face of God.

Nanael rules over the high sciences; he influences religious men, teachers, magistrates and men of law. The person born under this influence will possess a sedate demeanor; he will pursue a private life, rest and meditation, and he will distinguish himself through his knowledge of the abstract sciences.

Unconditional love opens all the doors of God. The Divine one can thus re-emerge in our daily living.

The negative side of this angel rules over ignorance and all bad characteristics of body and soul.

DECEMBER 15 TO DECEMBER 19

54. Nithael: The Angel of Kings"

Type: Principalities
Meaning: God King of the Skies

Attributes:

Nithael rules over emperors, kings, princes and all civilian and ecclesiastical dignitaries. He watches over all legitimate dynasties and over the stability of empires. Nithael is responsible for the long and peaceful reign to rulers who have a spiritual direction. This Angel and protects all those who wish to remain in their employment. The person born under this influence will become famous through his writings and eloquence.

He will have a strong reputation among scientists and will distinguish himself through his virtues and will gain the confidence of his leaders.

This Angel is associated with immortality and service towards humanity. The Angel Nithael guides us to discover true life, not egotistic life.

The negative side of this angel rules over the ruin of empires; he causes revolutions and overthrows; he influences all those who unite to overthrow governments for favored positions.

DECEMBER 20 TO DECEMBER 24

55. Mebaiah

Meaning: The Eternal God
Type: Principalities
Hebraic Translation: Mem Beit Hei Yod Hei

Attributes:

Mabaiah aids in obtaining consolation, compensaton, and for those who wish to have children. This angel rules over morality and religion; he influences those who protect them with all their power and spread them by all possible means. The person born under this influence will be distinguished by his good works, his piety and his zeal for completing his duties before God and man.

By meditating on this Angel you gain the power to reunite the Upper and Lower worlds. By uniting these realms, you will find courage and commitment to accomplish your goals and achieve your dreams. Your thoughts are achieved; your best ideas are manifested in action and then reality.

Angel Mebahiah teaches us quality and force that comes from words. It teaches us the magic of words, because if these words are connected to the conscience of love and the Light, they hold a great power. They then become words inspired by God, the Guides of Light and the Angels. When a work of high conscience enables us to connect the language of the Guides, we channel their vibrations by our voice. The voice is an unbounded transmitter which transforms and aids us in discovering all the possibilities and attaining your desired quality of life in the years to come. The voice transmits love and the Light of the Beings of Light.

The Angel Mebahiah, messenger of the love, makes anything beautiful. This Angel transmits the love that exploits several planes, and thus gives its energy to several levels; Thus all things bloom in their full potential.

The negative side of this angel is the enemy of virtue; he influences all those who wish to destroy religion and the princes who protect it, in order to prevent the great work of the regeneration of the human race.

DECEMBER 25 TO DECEMBER 29

56. Poiel: "The Angel of Divine Request"

Type: Principality
Meaning: God Who Supports the Universe

Attributes:

Poiel serves to obtain what one asks, for the fulfillment of one's requests. This angel rules fame, fortune and philosophy. It enables us to contemplate the things of the Life, and living within our community. The person born under this influence will be held in esteem for his modesty, moderation and a pleasant conduct.

By invoking this Angel anger is purged from your heart. Happiness and peace of mind come from within.

Angel Poiel is also the Angel which teaches to find the direction in our life as related to the Divine love. It gives us perseverance, tenacity and patience in any act of engagement and working to restore and reach balance in life.

Angel Poiel enables us to reach fortune and with abundance because it shows us this Wisdom, in our daily life and how to bear fruit with what we have in the material or spiritual elements. It helps us to live in affluence if we need some to achieve our work. It helps us to find all the elements necessary to build our own daily history making and shows us what prevents us from finding balance in our everyday. It leads us to live and experience each thing with balance and moderation, good mood and joy.

The negative side of this angel rules over ambition and pride; he influences all those who set themselves up as masters and wish to raise themselves above others.

DECEMBER 30 TO JANUARY 3

57. Nemamiah: "The Angel of Honor and Service

Type: ArchAngel
Meaning: Honorable Aspect of God

Attributes:

Nemamiah rules over great captains, admirals, generals and all those who fight for just cause. This Angel influences people who love the military state. They will distinguish themselves through their actions, bravery, spirit, and courage. Nemamiah's attribute is Praiseworthy God. He serves to bring prosperity in all areas and to deliver prisoners.

The being animated by Angel Nemamiah receives new, revolutionary ideas and feels the need to materialize these ideas. He gives us the right direction and clear vision of ourselves and those who surround us, thus enabling us to complete our tasks and know who we can count on.

Angel Nemamiah gives clarity on possessions and how to earness on wordly goods and how to respectfully/humbly manage them.

This Angel also opens all the infinite doors within us to discover the inner Light we hold. Angel Nemamiah helps us to find victory inside us and to reach the higher plane.

The negative side of this angel rules over treason, the cause of disagreement among leaders; he influences cowardly men and those who attack defenseless people.

JANUARY 4 TO JANUARY 8

58. Ieialel: "The Angel of Cures"

Meaning: The God Who Hears the Generations
Type: Archangel

Attributes:

Ieialel serves against disappointments and cures illnesses, principally problems with the eyes. You gain the courage to let go of everything; of all past, trauma, pain and suffering. He will be influenced by Venus/Love.

This angel rules over fire; he influences metal workers, ceramic workers and those involved in commerce.

Angel Ieialel allows us reconnect with the past for better living in the present, thus recognizing the future. It teaches us to stimulate these three energies and enables us to integrate the present like a tool of psychological displacement as a vehicle of Light.

This Angel has the knowledge of laws which govern the galaxies. Angel Ieialel speaks to us about the Universe and knows stars, planets and Cosmos.

The negative side of this angel rules over anger; he influences evil and homicides.

JANUARY 9 TO JANUARY 13

59. Harahel: "The Angel of Change"

Meaing: God Who Knows All Things
Type: Archangel

Attributes:

Harahel rules over treasures, agents of change, public funds, archives, libraries and all rare and precious collections. He influences printing, the book trade and all those involved in that business. Harahel's attribute is God Who Knows All Things. He serves against the sterility of women and to make children obedient and respectful towards their parents.

The person born under this influence will love all sciences in general; will follow the activities of the Stock Exchange and will speculate successfully and be distinguished by his integrity, talents and fortune.

Meditation on this name made for establish an umbilical cord to the Divine Energy, ensuring a constant glimmer of Light to your life, especially when you are in a place of darkness.

Angel Harahel is associated with a constant connection to Divine Energy. He enables us to discover the gift of balance so that each thing given and received is always in equilibrium. It enables us to discover the abundance which we possess and to live it and communicate it to any thing and any being. We understand that lack does not exist but that we create it. We are asked to share abundance her and now. We are also asked to give back to the rapture which first gave us this gift. Angel Harahel helps us to find the ingenuousness of the child who is not in need of anything since his/her parents provide and bring all which it needs.

The negative side of this angel rules over the enemies of illumination; he causes ruin and destruction through fire; he influences embezzlement and fraudulent bankruptcy (as opposed to systemically induced).

JANUARY 14 TO JANUARY 18

60. Mitzrael: "The Angel of Liberation"

Meaning: God Who Liberates the Oppressed
Type: Archangel

Attributes:

Mitzrael serves to heal spiritual ills and to be delivered from those who persecute us; he is the Liberator. Mitzrael rules over famous people who are distinguished by their talents and merits. He influences the commitment and compliance of subordinates towards their supervisors. The person born under this influence will unite all the qualities of body and soul and will have a long life.

Meditation on this Angel will bring balance and harmony that fills all Creation, especially in the hardships, challenges and tests that now you must face throughout life. You can muster the strength to pass all those tests, to rise to a higher level of being, and true spiritual transformation.

Angel Mitzrael teaches us how to become beautiful and balanced, to open up to others, while staying within our boundries and staying out of their bounderies while living exchanging love in it's fullest expression, with ourselves, harmony and our own nature. We learn how to become a servant to ourselves, of our body, our spirit and our conscience. Thus, we learn how to become a servant of the world.

Angel Mitzrael opens the doors of technologies in the space age to discover other worlds and other lives. These doors have been closed again because of the inconsistency human beings and its lack of opening, love and tolerance.

The negative side of this angel rules over all insubordinate beings, and influences all bad physical and moral qualities.

JANUARY 19 TO JANUARY 23

61. Umabel: "The Angel of Channels"

Meaning: God Above All Things
Type: Archangel

Attributes:

Angel Umabel is the Angel that channels the Word and wishes of God, he is a conduit. We are assisted in finding the courage to change our vibration levels and in this way find joy and transformation in the world of humans. We can then be used as transmitters of energy of the Light of God and a bridge between the Angelic plane and our plane of existence. We are used guides and an access road so that each one, each thing, each being can reach one another at any point or state of being. In this way this Angelic influence is like a ray of the Sun, a ray of Light which heats, gives Light and shows the Way.

This is the Angel of writers who transmit Light. Umabel communicates the energy of the Angels which attain material form and helps them to make the passage.

Umabel serves to obtain a person's friendship. This angel rules over astronomy and physics and influences all those who distinguish themselves in these fields. The person born under this influence will love travel, have a sensitive heart and love will cause him sorrows.

The negative side of this angel rules over the dissolute and particularly those who surrender themselves up to passions contrary to the order of nature.

JANUARY 24 TO JANUARY 28

62. Iah-hel: "The Guardian Angel of Children"

Meaning: The Supreme God
Type: Archangel

Attributes:

Angel Iah-Hel is the Guardian Angel of children. Iah-Hel is associated with the source of Divinity as a starting point of our incarnation. Angel Iah-Hel symbolizes the door of entry our being. Iah-Hel's attribute is God the Supreme Being. He serves to acquire wisdom.

During our formation in the womb, the child is in complete darkness. Upon birth, the Light becomes visible and takes form. This formation time is important because this is where the child reconnects within the interior darkness where it receives a multitude of information coming from the Earth and the Universe.

Iah-Hel is the key that assists in finding the Door of Time. This Door makes it possible to reach knowledge of the Life, Death and timelessness. Angel Iah-Hel makes us discover the unsuspected potentials which live within us.

This Angel harmonizes couples and makes them discover balance in living with each other. This Angel rules philosophers, enlightened ones and all those who are reclusive. The person born under this influence will love tranquility and solitude.

Angel Iah-Hel communicates with the Light which exists in our feminine side and helps us to find the balance of the feminine plane in all things.

The negative side of this angel rules over those who commit scandals; he rules over luxury, inconstancy and divorce; he provokes disunion between spouses.

JANUARY 29 TO FEBRUARY 2

63. Anauel: "The Gentle Angel"

ענו

Vav Nun Ayin
Affix/Nail + Fish/Humanity + Eye
"*Seeing Humanity and the Imprint of* G-d within it/us"
6 + 50 + 70 = 126 = 9 Gematria number

Meaning: The Gentle God
Type: Archangel

Attributes:

This Angel is infused with attributes of Moses. With these noble attributes one enjoys the blessings and treasures in life. Angel Anauel makes it possible to find the capacity of synthesis, reasoning, an overall picture and a globality of worldly things. It harmonizes our being as a whole while enabling us to accept as well our life on Earth and Heaven. It enables us to see that our existence as worthy in all planes.

Anauel teaches us diversity and the capacity to simultaneously offer our energy to many people, places or forms of energies and thereby benefit from the wealth of the possibilities of these energies.

This Angel protects against accidents, he preserves health and cures illnesses. He rules over commerce, bankers, businessmen and clerks. The person born under this influence will have a gentle, subtle and ingenious spirit.

Angel Anauel also teaches us that several beings live within us and that we can use their energies in order to better understand the Universe and discover all our relational possibilities. This is advantageous so we meet each situation easily to communicate what we have to say.

The negative side of this Angel rules over recklessness and wastefulnesss; he influences all those who are self destructive.

FEBRUARY 3 TO FEBRUARY 7

64. Mehiel: "The Heart Angel"

Meaning: The God who Energizes all things
Type: Archangel

Attributes:

This Angel represents the Heart of the World, the Heart of the Universe. It is the Heart of God that bubbles to the surface that pushes us toward the type of deep self evaluation where we will "see" God. It is your heart that energizes (like a pump) all things so that our spirituality has the capacity to be connected to all things.

Mehiel guards against adversities. Mehiel guides us to always live greater than what you are right now to be enable us to reach higher. He grants the prayers and wishes of those who hope within the mercy of God.

This angel protects against rabies and ferocious animals. He rules over the wise, teachers, orators and authors; he influences printing and bookshops and all those who engage in this type of business. The person born under this influence will distinguish himself in literature.

This Angel moves us communicate with our entire being by opening our mental doors, the doors of the thought and those of the world of creation.

The negative side of this angel rules over all counterfeit wise men; he influences controversies, literary disputes and criticism.

FEBRUARY 8 TO FEBRUARY 12

65. Damabiah: "The Wisdom Angel"

Meaning: God the Source of Wisdom
Type: Angel

Attributes:

Damabiah's attribute is God Fountain of Wisdom. This angel rules over seas, rivers, springs, maritime expeditions and naval construction; he influences sailors, pilots, fishing and all those for work in this line of commerce. Damabiah is associated to the symbolism of faith and "water," "the fish". He serves against sorcery and to attain wisdom and success in useful enterprises.

The person born under this influence will distinguish himself in marine affairs through his expeditions and discoveries, and he will amass a considerable fortune.

Angel Damabiah brings the cognizance of water which creates all things on Earth. Also, the Moon which moves open doors to Life that allows the blossoming of that Life; then to the Mother who produces Life--and thereby generates the Cosmos.

Angel Damabiah connects to us with the source of our intuition from our feminine side. It connects to us with the cellular life vibration, the first light of our being, and the Illumination of the Life that takes place by this integration of the masculine and the female characteristics.

The negative side of this angel causes storms and ship wrecks and influences unhappy expeditions.

FEBRUARY 13 TO FEBRUARY 17

66. Manakel: "The Nurture Angel"

Meaning: The God who nurtures and maintains
Every thing
Type: Angel

Attributes:

Menakel's attribute is the God Who Supports and
Nurtures All Things. He serves to appease God's
anger and to cure epilepsy. He rules over
vegetation and aquatic animals; he influences sleep
and dreams. The person born under this influence
will unite all the good qualities of body and soul; he
will bring about friendship and goodwill among all
good people through his appeal and the gentleness
of his character.

This Angel is associated with eradicating being the
victim, self pity and revenge. The notion of nurture
will heal and reassure us.

Angel Manakel brings us an unbiased perspective of ourselves which cultivates inner harmony within Time and Space. Our memory becomes a wonderful tool from the moment we acquire emotional detachment. If an event of feeling reminds us a wrong turn it is a great catalyst to modify our evolution. This builds a construction of humanity balanced in serenity, created from a deep experiment and finally wisdom.

Angel Manakel brings us the principles of the spiritual food which our body needs. When we undertake this change the spiritual food creates balance in our "body". This awakening brings radical changes in our way of living. A vibratory change brings a progressiveness that is accepting of humanity and releases in us a great charm and kindness.

The negative side of this angel rules over all bad physical and moral qualities.

FEBRUARY 18 TO FEBRUARY 22

67. Eiael: "The Angel of Youthfulness"

אִיעַ

Ayin Yod Aleph

70 + 10 + 1 = 81 = 9

"Seeing through the eyes of a Child, maintaining a youthful soul within a mature mind and body; i.e. keeping the soul open, and not holding on to trauma, burdens in the past, present or future to facilitate Joy, consequently the ability to mend, and move forward in a positive spiritual manner"

Meaning: G-d the pleasure of man's children

Type: Angel

Attributes:

Angel Eiael inspires a return to your youthful happiness and innocence which is combined with our current wisdom to grow, see and observe. In this way time time does not harden and youth is always present in us by the Life Force. This Life Force shows us our evolution and lessons in life.

Particularly for adults who learn how to look at life through the eyes of a child combined wih a mature mind.

Eiael is a key associated with water, to find Life. Eaiel serves to receive consolation in adversity and to acquire wisdom. This angel rules over change, the preservation of monuments and long life; he influences the spiritual sciences. The person born under this influence will become illuminated by the spirit of God; he will adore solitude and be distinguished in the high sciences, principally astronomy, physics and philosophy.

Angel Eiael puts to us in contact with harmony to take control of the course of our lifes and dispel the patterns which steals time so we can regain our course.

The negative side of this angel rules over error, prejudice and those who propagate flawed schemes.

FEBRUARY 23 TO FEBRUARY 28
ADAR 7 -12
Pisces
68. Habuhiah: "The Angel of Generosity"

חבו

Vav Bet Chet

$6 + 2 + 8 = 7$

*Root: bosom, inside, interior, xov

Embrace, affection, hidden concealed, hiding place, lair, retreat, beloved, secret place, hiding place
*Surround (like the surrounding of a cell) LIFE guarding, the vessel, as in man, the body, affix/nail/imprint; the concept of protecting humankind, the vessels, serving humanity, balancing life within the vessel. The nail, affix aspect of vav, as a "grounding" mechanism to stabilize the vessel, and Chet to cure/protect life.

Meaning: God Who Gives with Liberally

Type: Angel

Attributes:

Angel Habuhiah influences us to discover the
mother in us who is selfless, raises, educates,
protects, looks after and fights for his/her children.
These functions are there to give balance and to
guide to humanity. The energy of the mother shows
through with the need to be concerned about the
welfare of humankind and to revisit the concept of
service, charity and generosity as is typical of
"mother". Habuiah serves to preserve health and to
cure diseases.

Angel Habuhiah is also the Guard of Nature. This
angel rules agriculture and fertility. The person
born under this influence will love the countryside,
hunting, gardens and all things connected with
agriculture.

Meditate on this Angel to bring to mind memories
of loved ones who have passed on. See them
surrounded with the Light of this Angel and you
will open yourself up to receive their guidance and
support.

Angel Habuhiah aids in balancing dysfunctional energies on the instinctual and emotional levels to reach balance and serenity.

The negative side of this angel rules over sterility; he causes famine and plague; he influences insects which harm produce from the soil.

MARCH 1 TO MARCH 4

69. Rochel: "The Third Eye Angel"

Meaning: God Who Sees All
Type: Angel

Attributes:

Rochel serves to find lost or hidden objects, and to
know the person who has removed them. It enables
us to find the vision of God by love and the service.
It opens the door of the Third Eye by showing the
vision of knowledge and the Cosmic Laws.
This Angel influences jurisconsults, magistrates,
attorneys, solicitors and notaries.
This Angel is associated with your spiritual
compass that enables us to illuminate the path
towards your spiritual home. You regain direction
with assurance.

If we lost something, we can ask the Angel Rochel
why we lost it and how we can find it. It will
explain to us how to find balance.

Angel Rochel speaks to us about vision integrated with the material world in balance with Heaven and Earth and not experienced through deforming prism of the ego. He also speaks to us about pride which represents a major element of distortion of the vision of reality. The Angel Rochel also makes us work on illusions to better find the Light in our hearts.

The person born under this influence will be distinguished in law because of his knowledge of morality, custom and the intention of the law for all people. He rules fame, fortune and progression.

The negative side of this angel rules over reports, testaments and inheritances that are made to the detriment of legitimate inheritors. He influences all those who cause the ruin of families by predatory high fees and interminable court cases.

MARCH 5 TO MARCH 9

70. Jabamiah: "The Angel of Beauty"

Meaning: God Who Creates Everything with his
Word
Type: Angel

Attributes:

This Angel represents the peace found by the
abundance acquired by love and the love of
ourselves. Angel Jabamiah develops a very
thorough aesthetic direction. He makes all things
beautiful that are guided by the Planes of Light and
the healing of the heart.

Angel Jabamiah is the alchemist of our heart. The
call of beauty transforms the body. As our heart
lifts, it raises our body and our cells change. Thus
our body is prepared to receive new energies of
Light. Because it is the heart which always
transforms the body, makes it beautiful and closer
to God.

In this Light we can see the order beneath the chaos. You are enlightened to the Creator's master plan as it relates to your purpose in this world and to the problems you face.

Jabamiah rules over the evolution of beings and phenomena of Nature. The person born under this influence will be measured by the scientists of all the nations, and will become one of the first lights of philosophy.

The negative side of this angel rules over those who lack faith and all those who spread dangerous writings. He influences critics and literary disputes.

MARCH 10 TO MARCH 14

71. Haiaiel: "The Angel of Music and Prophecy"

Meaning: God, master of the Universe
Type: Angel

Attributes:

Angel Haiaiel brings us clairaudience which is the ability to experience Angelic influences through sound. He transmits to us the call of Angels within the subtle planes. It enables us to create in our conscience the type of music which accompanies us in our everyday life. It asks us to appreciate the music of the Angels in conjunction with the music which vibrates our emotional and our most primary instincts. It enables us to become aware of the importance of this music. These many sounds manifest in our environment and we choose what resonates within us.

Angel Haiaiel enables us to discover the energy of music that is connected to the Heavens. The music is the Light which takes action in the heart which becomes dynamic. Angel Haiaiel gives us the wisdom of listening which inspires silence in each of us so we can find the music within us. The music, the sound, the words create bridges of Light between Heaven and Earth. The music touches and makes it possible to communication with the very high vibratory planes of Angels which transcends matter and our cells.

Angel Haiaiel aids in communication with other planes, how to be receptive and creates the genesis of this type of communication. He brings new ways of receptivity and the tools that bring and facilitate these mechanisms.

This angel protects all those who call upon him; he gives victory and peace; he influences weapons, arsenals, fortresses and all connected with the military genius. The person born under this influence will have a lot of energy; love the military state and will be distinguished by his bravery, talents and actions.

Haiel is bestowed with the power of prophecy. With elevated consciousness you have the power to enter a new universe of transformation and Light.

The negative side of this angel rules over discord; he influences traitors and all those who become famous because of their crimes.

ADAR 24 TO ADAR 28 72nd NAME
APPROX: MARCH 15 TO MARCH 19

מ ו ם

MVM
Mem Vav Mem (final)
40 + 6 + 600 = Gematria of 7
Attributes:
Root word: Yod Mem. Yom The Red Sea, West;
westward
Mem as a preposition means from (me; me is G-d)
Mem Vav Mem; blemish, fault
This final sequence of the Name of G-d alludes to
the Red Sea now returning to it's original state.
Mem is the word for water, the Torah among other
meanings. As a component of MVM. G-d, the
"me" of the preposition of M (mem) has summoned
the Red Sea from the root word Mem Yod to return
to it's original "state" and directionally from the
west. When we started in the first few Names of G-
d, the East Wind was summoned to push the
waters/Red Sea to create a dry bed for the diaspora
to escape. Conversely, the west (wind) to return the
water to it's resting place.

Note the sequence from the 70th name of G-d the
diaspora was "cradled" in the palm of G-d across
the Red Sea. The 71st Name of G-d is the "voice"
of G-d, action from the Left Hand of G-d's severity
to now call the forces of nature to initiate the return
of the Red Sea which destroys Pharoah and his
army in the depths of the Red Sea.

Meditation: We have come full circle in this Name
of G-d. We are fully repaired and returned to our
state of Grace. After the fulfillment of the passage
through the Red Sea. All the fear, all the hardship,
all the miracles, repair us, and we are even better in
this new state of Grace, designed by the greated
designer of all time, The Master of the Universe, G-
d. We can find comfort is this Name that walking
in faith, moving forward, hard (or maybe easy for
some) we can be stronger, better more spiritual and
see the "big picture" of the intertwining of miracles,
struggles to reach Joy as our Creator has ordained.

72. Mumiah: "The Angel of Cleansing"

Meaning: God at the end of the Universe
Type: Angel

Attributes:

Angel Mumiah enables you rewind your spiritual
history. You will be cleansed in your present life
by correcting transgressions in your past lives. You
can also meditate on this Angel to purify your
physical environment from spiritual impurities.

This Angel has the capacity to create, illuminate,
give Life, and to restructure a cell. It knows the
secrets of the Earth, holds the energy of the 72
Angels and the 72 qualities of God. By experiment,
Mumiah has the gift to see and cure. He can make
cellular changes in conference with Divinity.

Angel Mumiah also represents the end of an energy
cycle which brings a revival, new births and the
foundation of a new era. It enables us best manage
this transition and to prepare us to what must come.
Mumiah also helps to discard/keep somebody or
something under control or within limits which
includes any work, any energy, any event or
relation/relationship which does not have any more
reason to exist in our lives and to embrace that thing
to be experienced or tested in its place.

This angel protects in mysterious operations; he brings success in all things and brings all things to their conclusion.

He rules over chemistry, physics and medicine; he influences health and longevity. The person born under this influence will be distinguished in medicine; he will become famous through his marvelous cures and will unveil many secrets of nature. This will lead to the prosperity of the children of earth, and he will devote his labors and his care to ease the poor and the sick.

Angel Mumiah shows us the material form of Life. All is becoming and dying to reappear at the same time. The Angel Mumiah makes us overcome any illusion and prepares us for illumination.

Angel Mumiah knows the secrecy of the Life. Because any object, any thing keeps an imprint of the place, people, events with which it was in contact. These imprints can be released from certain objects to find new joy and a new source of Light.

In the presence of disparity in relationships, The Angelic/Divine Correctio in the presence of events, relationships and elements that manifest and propogate disparity are: Despair and suicide; This correction can influence those who misunderstand their life and the day that they were born.

CHAPTER SIX

INDENTIFYING YOUR GUARDIAN ANGELS

Now once identified your three Guardian Angels are the code which has the potential to give eternal joy, peace, answers now, or at least most of the time. This is the Technology to analyze life past, present future because once you know the Angel Code you can recognize patterns in your life or other peoples lives in general. You can also use them in a scientific way to analyze world events in your own world or the Macro world in General. With that metaphysical knowledge we begin that internal/external conversation or analysis in our own minds, the ramifications of how we use this information for a greater good is endless.

Our Angels are at our disposal, from our birth, to help and support us throughout our existence.

One can determine very simply the name of your Guardian angels starting from the date and hour of birth. You will find initially your Angel Physical, then your Emotional Angel, finally your Spiritual Angel, all three charged to help you in their field. In the same way the requests can be made to them that correspond to their respective field.

Finding The Physical Guardian Angel

You will find the name of your Guardian angel of the physical plane thanks to your date of birth, because each Angel chairs five days consecutively of the year. All requests relating to that Angel will be able to relate to the material aspect of the life; physical health, problems financial, legal, organizational, professional, and lost objects.

The Emotional Guardian Angel

You also find your Emotional Guardian Angel according to your date of birth, but this Angel chairs five days nonconsecutive of the year. One will be able to ask for assistance in the relational, emotional and sentimental life. All problems concerning the control of our emotions like anger, the fear, hatred, or on the contrary concerning the development of certain feelings seldom expressed like the compassion, the affection, pity or to support sentimental relations.

The Spiritual Guardian Angel

You will determine it thanks to your hour of birth by taking into account the solar hour paying attention to the summer-time hours and the hours of winter! Also you must make calculation according to where you were born and re-calculate that into Greenwich time. For example if you were born in St. Louis at 5pm you would need to calculate what that would be in Greenwich Time. (Please see Spiritual Angel table for calculating your Angel). This Angel is devoted to our realization on the spiritual level, therefore with the improvement of the quality of our heart and with our ascension into higher spiritual realm in terms our Soul power.

CHAPTER SEVEN

How the Address the Guardian Angels

One can completely dialogue regularly with our three Guardian angels to present our requests, wishes, and hopes of all kinds to them and in order to obtain the realization of them.

There are several ways of contacting them: You can address one of your three Guardian angels, any time, because they are constantly at your disposal. You can, at a given time, to request the physical or emotional Angel which chairs the particular day in progress, or the twenty minutes the spiritual Angel is responsible for (keep in mind the hour calculation as per the Spiritual Angel table) during which you make your request. In this case, it is not an issue that the chairing Angel is not one of your personal Angels. You can refer to the Angel designated that is in charge of the day and the hour of your request.

For example, September 17 at 5pm, the three Guardian Angels which govern this moment are Mendel No. 36 on the physical plane, Haamiah No. 38 on the Emotional plane and Ariel No. 46 on the Emotional plane.

You can also address any one of the 72 Guardian angels because the of the attribute which is under their charge and/or the Angel Hierarchy to which it belongs has a relationship with your request. *For example* : - You will choose an Angel of **the Thrones** to help you when you are being tested or suffering.

You will choose an Angel of the **the Powers** to develop your personality and identity. You could call upon the Angel Achaiah No. 7 to know your destiny, your lifepath or to develop literary qualities and to discover the secrets of nature.

The Emotional, Spiritual and Physical Angels are specifically designed to "rule" over time, season, day, and hour. Needless to day many Angels are doing double, triple or quadruple duty. The following Tables, 1, 2, 3, and 4; each possess what Day, Month and Hour each Angel possesses and there you will derive your three Angels. Further you will possess the attributes of these Angels which give each individual their characteristic of the Emotional, Spiritual and Physical Worlds.

Whether you will refer to them as Angel signs or the Names or language of God--as I attuned my life to God and Angels, signs began to manifest everywhere. In my mind I'd ask a question of God and/or my guardian Angels, I would wait keenly aware of messages, numbers, words and/or actions that were all answers or guides. These manifestations come in everyday living. It could be a number that flashes 111 on the clock radio, on the TV on a license plate. You may see the number 40 which is the Hebraic equivalent of Mem (see Table 1) which means water the deeper meaning fountain of knowledge, under stream water, waves or water which is life--are you being told the significance of a moment, a person. Take note, study it later. Be aware of your surroundings and you'll see God through Angels talking to you. Are you at your wits end and you see a Fountain or see the word

Fountain, maybe God and your Angels are telling
you hold on, choose life, Mem—things will be
okay.

Another example, I was wrestling with whether to
take on a new job with a new bank in the builder
division. That day I saw 222 and 333 in sequences
all over my town. The meanings of 222 are
building upon the New. Building New Lives and a
New World. While 333 = Universal service
through the quickening of our One Being. I took
the job and was better for it. It wasn't my final
stop, but part of my ascension.

I had begun to seriously consider a vocation of
healing, with Angels and I was driving, I asked God
and my Angels are you really here can you heal me
and other people.. At that moment a truck whizzed
up in front of mine, it was a Wednesday and it was
written Rafael. Raphael (I'm spelling it the way I
was taught) is the Angel of healing. Was that my
answer? I knew I had to explore this greater and
also knew I could heal a lot of people with the study
and knowledge of Angels.

Another time in traffic, I was asking are Angels
real, again a huge truck crossed the intersection in
my direct view and it said Angelos. As I learned to
listen and ask the answers came undeniably and
within the activity I was engaged. Watching TV,
driving in traffic or listening to music.

God speaks in signs throughout ancient biblical
times.

I subscribe to the school of thought that the Eternal,
G-d is a great scientist. The Bible, especially when
read in the original texts of Hebrew or Amharic
posses a numerical code. The code for Angels
comes from the script in the bible and these Angels,
these codes as written by G-d could change the
course of your life, I had to know how, they were
found and how to access them. Not that G-d is
inaccessible; The Eternal is always there to listen to
teach, to guide. But it was also said these Angels
represented G-dly attributes about us and I thought
if I could tap into that, I reach my highest potential.
Besides, I had nothing to lose at this point, and right
now I was one of the heavy hearted, not hopeless,
not heart-broken, just confused and feeling alone

and without the strength to change the course of my life.

I was flirting with fatal thoughts and at the same time wanting to live. But with all the bad choices I had made, how was I to do that? I turned to the one thing that could occupy my mind, maybe distract me long enough to take that next breath and face that next morning. This was The Bible, or research in whatever form that may be. Because I needed one, the first looked thing I looked up was miracles, that's where I learned of the miracle code in Exodus when God delivered the Israelites and parted the Red Sea. In the original Hebrew text these were the 72 names of God, and also the 72 Angels derived names.

I thought maybe G-d was a great scientist who transcended time and space. And if G-d wrote the Bible to teach maybe I could find my redemption, ascension and salvation. Also the practice of meditation on these magic names and seeing, learning, speaking the words were the key to unlocking miracles.

I started my journey to Angels for one reason and one reason only, utter despair. I think everyone meets that day or a progression of days when life is too hard to live. You may not be the type who would take your own life, but we've all had those dark days when you say to yourself, my life is wasting me away, why oh why, Lord, or Creator, or whichever Name you choose to communicate with your belief of the highest power, am I here?. My heart aches, my body is failing me, and my world is crumbling before my very eyes. For me it was one Friday January 9, 2004 and I figured I didn't know where I would be in the next hour. It was 1:32 pm and I had just barely gotten out of bed. I had ignored my phone the entire day. I couldn't even bear to think of talking to anyone, I felt so disengaged.

I had past misdeeds to undo and needed time to travel spiritually to render my karma clean. I felt if there was a specific way to do this, maybe my Angels would listen to me and send word to God, this daughter was in great remorse, pain and regret but with vision and hope and assist me in making amends.

I wrote this book for those empty spaces of pain and wondering why I'm here, why do I experience the things I do. So instead of reaching for alcohol, drugs or people you don't really connect with, there is an internal spiritual technology you can access. I also had to realize I had been blessed in so many ways, with a family that stood by me in the most heinous of times, my best times, the times I smiled or laughed or forgot myself in the beauty of kindred. But during the daily grind of work and general living, I felt the lingering questioning whisper of why should I live, why do I live. And those times were getting more frequent and longer, and I could hardly sleep at night. Tonight in the midst of settling a lawsuit against myself, my family and a now defunct business, I laid in bed after work for about one hour, numbed myself with television, tears brimming to overflow down my cheeks and thought I've got eons of time ahead of me and the pain I feel from this business which ruined me, in a sense and put such financial demands on the family I was undone. I figured I could lie in bed, watch TV, feel totally sad and hopefully sleep into oblivion to forget this reality.

But I knew the possibility of a long night of a breaking heart would and could be my closest company. I went to my computer, at least to write of how I was feeling and to choose an Angel meditation. I wanted the Angel who could assuage my fears and comfort me. So I looked in my papers and found the ancient name to dispel my utter and complete dread. Jabamiah. The Angel which produces all things. This Angels helps to develop spirituality, develops courage and will, supports the capacity of understanding, recognizing the design beneath disorder. Meditation on this Angel, always as a messenger to God, will reveal the order that underlies the chaos. Jabamiah enlightens you to the Creator's master plan as it pertains to your purpose in this world and to the problems you face. So that night I went to sleep with Jabamiah name in my mind and at least rested.

You see, going through personal tragedy in my own life, I feared my apathy, it was like will I come to a day or some cross roads and just say, forget it, I'm done? Camille Maurine, in her book, Meditation Secrets for Women, said this, "If energy cannot be expressed or fulfilled, madness, illness, and even

death can provide a way out....Death, of course , is
the final way out, and sometimes it can seem like
the only exit from intolerable psychic pain. Suicide
expresses not just hopeless surrender, but the will to
be free. Paradoxically, so obviously self-destructive
a choice is also an unconscious act of power.
Sometimes suicide is a succinct display of unspoken
anger or resentment, reflecting a hidden self-
assertion." She goes on to say, "She [suicidal
person] can integrate the secret power, harness the
desire to be free, and bring that freedom into life."
Well, I didn't really want to go that route, so I
slogged on, writing as my passion, numbers my
love and spirituality my life.

I also knew that I would not be able to do the things
I aspired to do if I didn't get my emotions under
control.

How many times could I cry out an entire day,
wondering about my mother's death, why my father
had to die that way—and the fact, they were such
giving people and still somehow G-d's plan
included their relatively short lives and tragic
deaths. And here I was feeling so confused, what

chance did I have? And the most simple thing, deciding and marshalling up the nerve to have the energy to go work tomorrow so I could pay my mortgage and car note—and almost not caring at all, and caring just enough to tackle my demons through G-d's Angels. The joy maybe of personal self-sufficiency in my own skin that no one could take away.

What do I want? To be a full-time author, successful, fulfilled and self sufficient. To know what it's like to be sure about loving someone understand the desire to have children. To not feel fear or dread. To know the Eternal is really there and that G-d's spark of life when I listen to it can save me. To be healthy. To not need doctor prescribed medicine just to sleep at night. To love myself as I am and the ability to change the things I can and accept what I cannot. To be fearless. To do Elohim's work, to challenge my re-born soul, and all the kharma I've absorbed and redeem my transgressions. So this next life time around I'll be a better soul.

This technology is for all kinds of people. The people with a tenuous hold on life. When there's no one else besides your Creator, your Angels and yourself. For that extra moment in time you need to go on one more minute, which turns into one more day and finally one more year. And as I write this as a work in progress myself struggling with life and living and the what's it all about and why's, I live another day to find solace to find love when I feel so troubled and unloveable because my life is such a mess. I write these words to save my own life and I can only tell you, if I finish it, get it to be published then it was true. Miracles really do happen, God is real and Angels listen and are God's messengers. Because as I sit at this computer in a planet full of war, discrimination and unGodliness it's easy for me to feel overwhelmed by negativity and sorrow.

This is also for the Strong, the re-affirmation of your path. Or, maybe you're bringing new life into this world and when you decipher this new life's Angels you can have a glimpse of the positive attributes of their future and encourage them. Or just need a miracle—but as with any technology you must understand the under layers of it. The basics, G-d is to be worshipped, not Angels, they are a manifest of G-dly attributes. This technology is for the light and a true interest in ascension. Understanding the planet, the universe is for all to enjoy and grow and your goals are positive in nature.

I studied on. I learned the proper names of Angels hold great mystical and magical power. There are three verses in Exodus (as stated earlier) each containing seventy-two letters. By writing down the first of these, and underneath this the next verse backward, and under this again the last verse forwards, 72 columns of three letters each are obtained. These are read downwards and the terminations "al" or "ah", according as they are male or female, appended. There is also an attribution of these intelligences, one to each of the quinaries or segments of five degrees of the zodiac; but there are also innumerable other angels, demons, magical images, lords of triplicities, lesser assistant angels and so on , with demons to correspond. It is well to bear in mind that all angels whatever their state of grace, indeed, no matter how christologically corrupt and defiant - are under god, even when, to all intents and purposes, they are performing under the direct orders of the devil. Evil itself is an instrumentality of the creator, who uses evil for his own divine, if unsearchable, ends. Angels perform a multiplicity of duties and tasks. Preeminently they serve god. They also carry out missions from G-d to man. But many serve man directly as guardians, counselors, guides, judges, interpreters, cooks, comforters, match- makers and gravediggers.

Most angel names in Judaic-Christian lore are Hebrew. The "-el" at the end of the names is a suffix meaning "God;" thus angels are "of God."

I may repeat the derivation of Angels to keep us on track. Again, the 72 Guardian Angels, derived from Exodus14; Verses 19,20 and 21. When read in the traditional Hebrew the letters represent a miracle code that saved the Israelites and parted the red Sea. The words are also referred to as the 72 names of G-d in the most strictest translation, however with the addition of "el" or "ah" at the end of each code you thereby manifest an attribute of each one of the

72 angels. On a deeper level, the invocations of these ngels are a complement of God's code. For this, the knowledge of Angel names is magical, numerical and scientific.

Let's review, translated in English the Verses are as follows:

Verse 19

God's angel had been traveling in front of the Israelite camp, but now it moved and went behind them. The pillar of clouds thus moved from in front of them and stood at their rear.

Verse 20

It came between the Egyptian and the Israelite camps. There was cloud and darkness that night, blocking out all visibility. All that night [the Egyptians and Israelites] could not approach one another

Verse 21

Moses extended his hand over the sea. During the entire night, God drove back the sea with a powerful east wind, transforming the sea bed into dry land. The waters were divided.

In Hebrew each verse has 72 letters and when combined as 1st letter of the 1st verse, with the 1st letter of the 2nd verse, and the 1st letter of the third verse, creating a three letter code which are also designated as the 72 names of God, extrapolated further become the 72 names of the Guardian Angels. Coded derivatives of the miracle of the parting of the Red Sea and the role of God and Angels.

For this reason, I would suggest all people learn ancient languages such as amharic or Hebrew which are the original languages that were then translated to what is the Bible and Koran. As an aside, I believe it is a benefit for all peoples to learn other languages be it African languages, which are among some of them of the most ancient and also latin, french and/or spanish. I advocate the pursuit of other languages not only as a global benefit, but a intellectual enhancement of our people.

At my most solitary times brought on by many tribulations, my ability to immerse myself in Angel codes, Angel magic saved me. If not to say, when there appears to be nothing in your corner, there are these precious messengers to God who are always there at any hour or any day. Unlike human attachments, which are important, but temporary in the physical sense.

CHAPTER EIGHT

How Do People Experience the presence of Angels?

The experience of perceiving an angel with one or more of the five senses is called an "angelophany." Our present interest in angels has created an intense desire on the part of many people for angelophanies.

The angels do their best to get our attention and to communicate with us. In this way, they help us heal our own lives. However, we often discount the signs they give us, writing them off as mere coincidences or our imagination. The angels say: "We can't write our messages to you in the sky. You've got to pay attention and believe when you see any patterns forming in your life - especially in response to any questions or prayers you've posed. When you hear the same song repeatedly or see the same number sequence, who do you think is behind this? Your angels, of course!"

This study of angels had most to do with my on-going survey of religion. To answer all those questions we have about birth, death, suffering and pain. As I got deeper in the annals of the bible, the torah, the koran and all other beliefs I came upon angels. My first impression was the guardian Angels. An army of Names, attributes and "jobs" carried out for the human race and God. This was interesting to me. Then I thought well do I have particular angels assigned to me as an individual and do others as well. Furthermore, if I learned these Angels' names would they give me a clue as to why I am the way I am and could I speak to them. I always felt I had "protectors". Even as bad as things had gotten in my life, I felt they could be much worse and much better, but I just didn't have the knowledge of how to harness this power. Many times I could have died and didn't, but also I had lost parents at a relatively young age in my twenties and early thirties, and I felt that loss deeply and couldn't quite wrap my mind around it's significance. Other than age old adage, that a certain amount of loss and suffering is essential in building character, humility and grace. I knew that to be true, because of those very sad moments of my parent's death I did learn lessons. Lessons that life is ephemeral, unpredictable. How someone dies can have lasting impressions on how to live your life a little smarter. I got even closer to my siblings. And I was learning more about myself, my hopes, dreams, ambitions, fears, my strengths, my shortcomings.

So who were these protectors within the Godly realm? Would I benefit by studying them further apart from just knowing "they were there" with me somehow? Aside from the fact I loved to read and ction Page | 242

just going through the motion of Angelic study was
interesting in itself.

Some say our need to believe in angels is our
recognition of the need to look at the world in a
more spiritual way.

The world's great literature and art tell us about
many Angel characters - some we're familiar with
and some obscure to us now. Yet, the common
thread that weaves amongst the legends and the lore
is the undeniable influence that angels have had
upon nearly every culture and religion known to
man.

Hebrew concepts formed the background for
Christian beliefs concerning heaven and angels.
Some scholars say that the earliest religious
representation of an angel was found at Ore, the
Sumarian capital of the Hebrews. A winged figure
is shown descending from heaven to pour water
from an overflowing jar into the cup held by a king.
Others suggest the earliest depiction of an Angel is
found in the annunciation scene at the catacombs of
Priscilla in Rome dating from the 2nd century AD.

But archaeological remains of the earliest Christian church found in Syria that was built or remodeled in 233 AD shows no pictures of angels. A synagogue found in the same spot however shows robed figures attending Moses. For the early Christian church, the time of the Angels had not yet come. It wasn't until the reign of Constantine the Great from 306 to 337 AD that Christian art began to flourish and then we began to see the characteristic appearance of Angels.

One interesting thing I learned was they didn't look like how I had been indoctrinated to see them. Earlier in this book we revealed the actual description taken from ancient texts, like the Bible, the Torah, etc. Their descriptions were almost fearsome, but within that spirit, I found comfort because Angels had to be strong. Strong enough to fight the darkness and other fallen Angels. And those fallen Angels were architects of despair, hatred and hopelessness. If I needed an Angel to do battle for me, I wanted that Angel of God to be fearsome to behold and to do battle with. So with this knowledge I began to fear less unknown monsters of spiritual destruction, because according to Angel descriptions, God's Army of spiritual construction were just as fierce in duties.

Angels for me were beings to hold on to, a support I could depend on, when there was no one else. Because just as my parents had died, I knew those closest to me could also pass on and I would be left alone with myself, My Creator and My Angels. In this sense it helped conquer my dread of being truly alone. But as we all know, in the middle of the day, in the cool of the night, no matter who's laying next to you, sitting beside you, your thoughts are your own and what will they manifest without knowledge of self and more importantly knowledge of ancient belief and how we got here.

I mean as we sit at our jobs, or in our homes, where do our thoughts lie. Is it enough to think about what's on TV tonight, what will I eat, how will I lose those ten pounds, or should I be trying to make the world a better place by knowing things, people, places, books and the pursuit of art, science and spirituality. For me it was the latter, art, science and spirituality, and the study of Angels embodied all that.

An art, because of the esoteric nature of Angelogy, a science because Angels had particular names, numerical values, connected to cosmology, astrology and more charts than you can imagine. Spiritual because as we learn their essences they can perform miracles in the physical, emotional and spiritual worlds as written in the most Ancient text of all, The Bible the written by the master Scientist of all time, G-d.

I also felt profoundly that humankind was becoming more cynical and our goals were being dominated by selfishness. The fight between religious sects was superficial. The desire for domination by different groups was shocking and our dependence on substances, food, drink, TV and less on learning was lamentable. Most network news was fact based on fiction, and I could not believe in the second millennium, we were still saying Johnny doesn't read, Jane is overweight because she plays video games and eats fast food. Statistics said the majority of people believe in Angels, so we still had hope, but what did they believe about them and what did they know. This book is an introduction to the basics of Angelogy.

Why bother, some say, God is enough, yes, but many schools of thought say the Bible is a Code andAngels are part of that code. If God did write this code, is it not worth it to at least contemplate it's meaning, And maybe the meaning of life?

Now how many are there, what do they do, do we all have personal Angels and what is their relationship to God.

I was never the type to go to meetings or counseling groups; I gritted my teeth and attacked my own problems in my solitude. Well maybe that wasn't right, but I was sort of brought up in a civilized world where we kept our voices down and studied.

I feel a major point of similarities with us all is understanding death why we may lose a brother, mother, child or father early on. Whether it is by divorce, a legality issue, an accident, cars and such, assassinations, suicide, murder we ask God, why me? The propensity for the status quo to maintain

the status quo in it's many forms, but basically
identical in it's construct makes us rail against the
machine. In so doing, we smoke, we drug, we
drink, and we question ourselves by other people's
rules. Well, Godly and Angelic rules are the
primary rules, there are no other. And being able to
interpret those rules are our own God given right.
Not necessarily what your minister says, what your
politician says, but what God says and Angels as
constructs of those messages. It's inner work,
probably more important than any other work we
must do.

And as I got dressed every morning to go to a job I
barely wanted to go to, I felt the hoplessness of my
life. I was always asking why. Why was I born to
be so imperfect. Are my imperfections threatening
to end my life sooner from stress, from self-doubt
from apathy and depression?. And I'm cramping up
from my monthly cycle having to take painkillers
which make me tired and I don't want to leave my
house, save I must somehow make money to pay
my mortgage, my car note and I pretend to live, I
pretend to want to be alive and all the while living
through this fake life I'm wondering why? I fell so

expendable, but I don't want to. I want to have a purpose, but as far as I know I have none. Save this book, my desire to look into time and space and find meaning from myself for all of us here on this universe. But as time ticks by it seems more and more elusive, sometimes I get a glimpse but is dissipates in thin air.

So, I figured I would go into counsel with the Angels. Because from what I understood, this is what they were supposed to be:

Messengers
Healers
Miracle workers
Could talk to God for you
Were not to be worshipped only God was

The major thing I set about doing was finding my guardian Angels and If possible their names.

I wrote this book to give definitive research to Angels and in-depth information about how they relate to our lives. The richness of the study of Angels in deep and powerful.

And if for one thing, the power they emanate can give a person in times of happiness or sorrow and the one unwavering thing as a manifestation of God that gives comfort.

And one of my biggest reasons was how to tap into the miracle that would rid the world of AIDS/HIV. This deadly disease that was killing millions. Could I pray enough to God and the Angels to find a solution to this problem that humankind had been diluted to money vs. lives. As I sat here writing, healthy, I was truly blessed by Hashem, because I knew we were all susceptible to this killer, so if I had breath in my body, I had been spared, given a chance to live for some reason, if only to get closer to The Eternal, live this life as well as I could and understand the Universe, that was enough.

What was also really important and I find this is true for those of us who have lost parents through either death, divorce or absence is that you need to do things for your own, or better yet the Creator's fulfillment. Many times you reach pinnacles in life where there may be no one to share it with and that hollowness can consume you rather than if you do it for a magical, esoteric, karmic, Godly reason that transcends reality. Angels were my touchstone to this esoteric existence where I didn't necessarily need a cheering squad or anyone to acknowledge my contributions or lack there of. Sometimes this lead me to a very solitary existence and it would be hard to pull me out for any kind of physical interaction with anybody for long periods of time. I found it necessary to make that soul connection with God because my incessant question was what is it all about?

And I had spent my lifetime thus far, watching people, reading books just to answer that question. And I knew for my own life if I could not get that answer my ability to survive would be compromised.

CHARTS AND TABLES

TABLE 1

The Final Table the adds the Hebrew letters EL and AH which means "God of" or "of God" as Angels are aspects of God you now derive the 72 Holy Angel names which will be utilized to find your three Guardian Angels.

TABLE 2

First Verse Exodus 19

וַיִּסַּע מַלְאַךְ הָאֱלֹהִים הַהֹלֵךְ לִפְנֵי מַחֲנֵה יִשְׂרָאֵל וַיֵּלֶךְ מֵאַחֲרֵיהֶם
וַיִּסַּע עַמּוּד הֶעָנָן מִפְּנֵיהֶם וַיַּעֲמֹד מֵאַחֲרֵיהֶם:

God's angel had been traveling in front of the Israelite camp, but now it moved and went behind them. The pillar of cloud thus moved from in front of them and stood at their rear.

מ	מ	ע	א	שׁ	ל	א	ו	1
ד	פ	ע	ח	ר	פ	ל	י	2
מ	נ	מ	ר	א	נ	ה	ס	3
א	י	ו	י	ל	י	י	ע	4
ח	ה	די	ה	ו	מ	ס	מ	5
ר	ב	ה	ם	י	ח	ה	ל	6
י	ו	ע	ו	ל	נ	ה	א	7
ה	י	נ	י	ר	ה	ל	ר	8
ם	ע	ו	ס	מ	י	ר	ה	9

TABLE 3

Second Verse Exodus 20

וַיָּבֹא בֵּין מַחֲנֵה מִצְרַיִם וּבֵין מַחֲנֵה יִשְׂרָאֵל וַיְהִי הֶעָנָן וְהַחֹשֶׁךְ וַיָּאֶר
אֶת הַלָּיְלָה וְלֹא קָרַב זֶה אֶל זֶה כָּל הַלָּיְלָה:

It came between the Egyptian and the Israelite camps. There was
cloud and darkness that night, blocking out all visibility. All that night
[the Egyptians and Israelites] could not approach one another.

8	7	6	5	4	3	2	1
ה	ס	ל	ה	ל	י	ל	ה
ק	ר	ב	ו	ה	א	ל	ז
ה	ל	י	ל	ה	ו	ל	א
ש	ך	ו	י	א	ר	א	ת
י	ה	ע	נ	ן	ו	ה	ו
י	ש	ר	א	ל	ו	י	ה
ו	ב	י	ו	מ	ח	נ	ה
ח	נ	ה	מ	צ	ר	י	ם
ו	י	ב	א	ב	י	ו	מ

TABLE 4

Third Verse Exodus 21

וַיֵּט מֹשֶׁה אֶת יָדוֹ עַל הַיָּם וַיּוֹלֶךְ יְהוָֹה אֶת הַיָּם בְּרוּחַ קָדִים עַזָּה כָּל
הַלַּיְלָה וַיָּשֶׂם אֶת הַיָּם לֶחָרָבָה וַיִּבָּקְעוּ הַמָּיִם:

Moses extended his hand over the sea. During the entire night, God
drove back the sea with a powerful east wind, transforming the sea bed
into dry land. The waters were divided.

י	ה	י	י	ה	ו	ד־	ו	1
ב	י	ל	מ	י	ל	ו	י	2
ק	ם	ה	ע	ב	ר	ע	ט	3
ע	ל	ו	ז	ב	י	ל	מ	4
ו	ח	י	ה	ר	ה	ה	ש	5
ה	ר	ש	ס	ו	ו	י	ה	6
מ	ב	ב	ל	ח	ה	ם	א	7
י	ה	א	ה	ק	א	ו	ת	8
ב	ו	ת	ל	ד	ת	י	י	9

TABLE 5

Completed Chart from Verses that derive the 72
Miracle Code Angels

כדהת	אכא	ללה	מהש	עלם	סיט	ילי	והו
הקם	הרי	מבה	יזל	ההע	לאו	אלד	הזי
וזהו	מלה	ייי	נלך	פהל	לוו	כלי	לאו
ושר	לכב	אום	ריי	שאה	ירת	האא	נתה
ייז	רהע	חעם	אני	מנד	כוק	להח	יוו
מיה	עשל	ערי	סאל	ילה	וול	מיכ	ההה
פוי	מבה	נית	ננא	עמם	החש	דני	והו
מוחי	ענו	יהה	ומב	מצר	הרח	ייל	נמם
מום	היי	יבמ	ראה	חבו	איע	מנק	דמב

TABLE 6
The Angel Names
The 72 Angels in Numerical Order of the 360 degree Angelic (Angle) Circle

ANGELS	Number	ANGELS	Number
VEHUIAH	1	ANIEL	37
JELIEL	2	HAAMIAH	38
SITAEL	3	REHAEL	39
ELEMIAH	4	IEIAZEL	40
MAHASIAH	5	HAHAHEL	41
LELAHEL	6	MIKAEL	42
ACHAIAH	7	VEUALIAH	43
CAHETHEL	8	IELAHAIAH	44
HAZIEL	9	SEALIAH	45
ALADIAH	10	ARIEL	46
LAUVUEL	11	ASALIAH	47
HAHAIAH	12	MIHAEL	48
IEZALEL	13	VEHUEL	49
MEBAHEL	14	DANIEL	50
HARIEL	15	HAHASIAH	51
HAKAMIAH	16	IMAMIAH	52
LAUVIAH	17	NANAEL	53

CALIEL	18	NITHAEL	54
LEUVIAH	19	MEBAIAH	55
PAHALIAH	20	POIEL	56
NELCHAEL	21	NEMAMIAH	57
IEIAIEL	22	IEIALEL	58
MELAHEL	23	HARAHEL	59
HAHIUIAH	24	MITZRAEL	60
NITH-HAIAH	25	UMABEL	61
HAAIAH	26	IAH-HEL	62
IERATHEL	27	ANAUEL	63
SEHEIAH	28	MEHIEL	64
REIIEL	29	DAMABIAH	65
OMAEL	30	MANAKEL	66
LECABEL	31	EIAEL	67
VASARIAH	32	HABUHIAH	68
IEHUIAH	33	ROCHEL	69
LEHAHIAH	34	JABAMIAH	70
CHAVAKIAH	35	HAIAIEL	71
MENADEL	36	MUMIAH	72

CHAPTER TEN

The Angel Hierarchy

The basic hierarchy of angel is as follows:

Highest Triad

Seraphim

The Seraphs are generally accepted to be the highest order of God's Angelic Servants. They stand by God's throne chanting *"Kadosh, Kadosh, Kadosh"* - "Holy, Holy, Holy is the Lord of Hosts, the whole earth is full of His Glory." (Isaiah 6:3) They are beings of pure light and thought and have direct communication with God. They resonate with the Fire of Love. They appear with six wings and four heads.

According to Enoch, there were only 4 Seraphim, which corresponded to the four winds or directions. Later commentators interpreted this as there were 4 major princes who ruled over the Seraphim. They include either Metatron or Satan, Kemuel, Nathanael, and Gabriel.

Certain passages also refer to a saraph or Seraphim as "fiery serpents" (*saraph* means fiery) - see Numbers 21:6 and 21:8, Deuteronomy 8:15, and several passages in Isaiah. Isaiah 30:6 talks of a "fiery flying serpent" which lives in the southern desert between Palestine and Egypt. Isaiah 6 is the only reference in the Bible to the Seraphim which does not identify them as serpents. Here they are described as standing "in attendance on Him. Each of them had six wings: with two he covered his face, with two he covered his legs, and with two he would fly." (Isaiah 6:2).

It is possible that the earlier passages refer to a class of demons. Another interpretation is that the word comes from *rapha* meaning healer and *ser* meaning higher being.

There is much confusion in the ranks of angels. Some of the Seraphim are considered Archangels, even though the Archangels are ranked six orders below that of the Seraphim.

Metatron is sometimes identified as Satan, Prince of
Darkness, or "old dragon." He is said to possess 36
wings and countless eyes. **"Seraphim** stood above
Him, each having six wings; with two he covered
his face, and with two he covered his feet, and with
two he flew". Isaiah 6:2

Cherubim

Cherubim are represented as guardians with many
wings. Thrones have been depicted wearing stoles
and kneeling before God.

These Cherubim had the faces of the beings which
were in the four cardinal points of the Zodiac, when
the Bull was the equinoctical sign, viz. The ox, the
lion, the man, and the eagle.[1]

Genesis 3:24 says of that God placed "on the east
side of the Garden of Eden cherubim and a flaming
sword flashing back and forth to guard the way to
the tree of life."

---

[1] Anacalypsis, Godfrey Higgins

The Hebrew word *Kerub* is translated by some scholars as "one who intercedes" and by others as "knowledge." The original *Karibu* were the terrible and monstrous guardians of the temples and palaces in Sumer and Babylon. There were also similar guardians in the Near East, and there were winged, eagle-headed deities that guarded an Assyrian Tree of Everlasting Life. They are said to have 4 wings and 4 faces. Exodus 25 talks of how the Ark was to be decorated with Cherubim, while 1 Samuel 4:4 says that the Lord is "enthroned between the cherubim" on the Ark. Psalms 18:10 speaks of the Lord, who "mounted the cherubim and flew; he soared on the wings of the wind."

Ezekiel describes them as such: "They had the figures of human beings. However, each had four faces, and each of them had four wings; the legs of each were [fused into] a single rigid leg, and the feet of each were like a single calf's hoof; and their sparkle was like the luster of burnished bronze. They had human hands below their wings. The four of them had their faces and their wings on their four sides. Each one's wings touched those of the other. They did not turn when they moved; each could only move in the direction of any of its faces. Each of them had a human face [at the front]; each of the four had the face of a lion on the right; each of the four had the face of an ox on the left; and each of the four had the face of an eagle [at the back]. Such were their faces. As for their wings, they were separated: above, each had two touching those of the others, while the other two covered its body." - Ezekiel 1:5-11

Thrones (Ophanim or Galgallin)

The Ophanim seem to be God's actual chariots. The Hebrew *Galgal* has the double meaning of wheels and of "pupil of the eye." Ezekiel 1:13-19 "with them was something that looked like burning coals of fire. This fire, suggestive of torches, kept moving about among the creatures; the fire had a radiance, and lightning issued from the fire. Dashing to and fro [among] the creatures was something that looked like flares. As I gazed on the creatures, I saw one wheel on the ground next to each of the four-faced creatures. As for the appearance and structure of the wheels, they gleamed like beryl. All four had the same form; the appearance and structure of each was as of two wheels cutting through each other.

And when they moved, each could move in the direction of any of its four quarters; they did not veer when they moved. Their rims were tall and frightening, for the rims of all four were covered all over with eyes. And when the creatures moved forward, the wheels moved at their sides' and when the creatures were borne above the earth, the wheels were borne too."

The thrones are said to reside either in the third or the fourth heaven. They are said to inhabit a region in which Heaven meets Earth. Raphael is thought to be the ruling Prince.

The Second Triad

The Domininons

These angels are said to "regulate angels' duties" according to Dionysius. They are described as Dominions, Lords, Kuriotetes, or Hashmallim. They have been said to reside in the second heaven, where the celestial letters of the Holy Name reside. The ruling Princes are said to be Zadkiel, Hashmal (aka Chasmal or the "fire speaking angel"), Yahriel, and Muriel.

The Virtues

These angels bestow blessings, usually in the form
of miracles. They are also known as Malakim,
Dunamis, and Tarshishim. They are associated with
heroes and instill courage, and are known as "The
Brilliant or Shining Ones."
The Virtues escorted Christ to Heaven during the
Ascension and according to the *Book of Adam and
Eve*, were present at the birth of Cain.
The leaders are said to be Michael, Gabriel,
Raphael, Bariel, Tarshish, and Satanel (before his
fall).

The Powers

The Powers are also known as the Dynamis, the
Potentiates, and the Authorities. They are said to be
the first angels created by God, and are said to
reside along the border between the first and second
heavens. Their job is to guard against demons.
Camael is the leader of the order. His name means
"he who sees God" and the *Magus* suggests that he
is one of the seven angels who stands in the
Presence of God. Camael is also identified as a
Duke of Hell. He is said to have the body of a
leopard.

Others believe him to be associated with Mars, the god of war. He also is commander of Destruction, Punishment, Vengeance, and Death. As Kemuel, he acts as a mediator between Israel and the Hierarchs of the seventh heaven.

Legends surrounding Camael claim it was he who wrestled with Jacob, he appeared to Jesus in the Garden of Gethsemane, and even that he tried to prevent Moses from receiving the *Torah* from God.

The Powers are said to be the angels who guide the soul. They try to balance the good with the bad in hopes that the bad will not overpower the good, and hence, the individual will fall to the darker side. It is also said that they guide souls that have left the body and have lost their way.

The Third Triad

The Principalities

Principalities protect nations and their leaders. They are responsible for seeing to it that no one group of people are wiped completely off the earth. Each nation is assigned a guardian angel by God. These individual guardians are called Ethnarchs. Archons are also considered protectors of nations.

The archangels Gabriel, Michael, Raphael and Uriel are in this order. The Principalities are those angels who are in charge of nations and great cities on Earth. Later they became the protectors of religion. Several possible leaders are Nisrock, who is originally an Assyrian deity who sometimes is considered the chief chef to the Demon Princes of Hell. Another possible chief is Anael, who is one of the seven angels of creation. He is associated with human sexuality, and is also governor of the second heaven. Other Principalities include Hamiel, who transported Enoch to Heaven (although he is also known as the Chaldean deity Ishtar) and Cervill, the Prince of Strength, who is said to have aided David when he slew Goliath.

The Archangels

In Jewish and Christian sources, there are seven Archangels, while in the Koran, there are said to be only four - only two are named: Jibril (Gabriel) and Michael. The Jewish and Christian sources differ in who they name as their seven. All agree on Michael, Gabriel, Raphael, and Uriel. The other three are either Metatron, Remiel, Sariel, Anael, Raguel, and Raziel. These angels are the most important intercessionaries between God and humans, and they are in constant battle with the Sons of Darkness.

The Angels

The last order of the hierarchy is that of the Angels. The Hebrew term for angel, *mal'akh* means "a messenger, while the Sanskrit is *Angeres*, which becomes the Persian *angaros* ("courier"), and finally, the Greek *angelos*. They are intermediaries between God and human mortals.

Angels - Beings closest to the material world and serve as holy messengers between humans and God. They intercede taking our prayers to God and return with the answers. They are our guardians, protectors and minister to our needs. They may appear to humans in many different forms. They posses great power and can inspire both fear and awe in those they come in contact with. Sons of Life or Twilight.

CHAPTER 11

What Angels Really Look Like!

One of the things I learned about the appearance of Angels and God for that matter was the appearance, the cherubs, the women with wings were not the holy essence of Angels. Their true description is as formidable as the jobs they under take. I believe for most of us we have been bombarded with images of Angels which do not accurately describe their place in our lives, how they appear and that in itself is a great disservice. I will describe to you each level of Angel and their appearance, if not to set the record straight, but to encompass the power of these other worldly beings.

The Seraphim

They are beings of pure light and thought and have direct communication with God. They resonate with the Fire of Love. They appear with six wings and four heads.

Cherubim

They are said to have 4 wings and 4 faces. They had the figures of human beings. However, each had four faces, and each of them had four wings; the legs of each were [fused into] a single rigid leg, and the feet of each were like a single calf's hoof; and their sparkle was like the luster of burnished bronze. They had human hands below their wings. The four of them had their faces and their wings on their four sides. Each one's wings touched those of the other. They did not turn when they moved; each could only move in the direction of any of its faces. Each of them had a human face [at the front]; each of the four had the face of a lion on the right; each of the four had the face of an ox on the left; and each of the four had the face of an eagle [at the back]. Such were their faces. As for their wings, they were separated: above, each had two touching those back]. Such were their faces. As for their wings, they were separated: above, each had two touching those of the others, while the other two covered its body." - Ezekiel 1:5-11

Thrones (Ophanim or Galgallin)

"Many eyed ones
The Ophanim seem to be God's actual chariots. As I gazed on the creatures, I saw one wheel on the ground next to each of the four-faced creatures. As for the appearance and structure of the wheels, they

gleamed like beryl. All four had the same form; the appearance and structure of each was as of two wheels cutting through each other. And when they moved, each could move in the direction of any of its four quarters; they did not veer when they moved. Their rims were tall and frightening, for the rims of all four were covered all over with eyes. And when the creatures moved forward, the wheels moved at their sides' and when the creatures were borne above the earth, the wheels were borne too."

The Dominions

Fire speaking Angel. They look most like Humans.

The Virtues

The Angels

Know as the The Brilliant or Shining Ones. They may appear to humans in many different forms.

CHAPTER TWELVE

Angel Jobs

Angel Hierarchies:

SERAPHIMS: They develop the will and purify the sins. They help us to know our destiny according to the universal laws.

CHERUBIMS: They help us to find a medium favorable for our spiritual development. They contribute to transmit wisdom to those who wish it.

THRONES: They help us to analyze our life tests by explaining our course of direction. They help us to overcome our sufferings.

DOMINIANS: They contribute to develop our optimism, our joy, our kindness and dispense grace. They improve our self-confidence, confidence in the others and God.

VIRTUES: They help to establish justice and allow us to become "knights without fear and reproach", the anguish impending future and the remorse of the past. They strengthen us to face our tests.

POWERS: They enable us to discover our true identity and contribute to releasing us from external conditioning and to develop our own free will, i.e. strength.

PRINCIPALITIES: They sensitize us with the beauty of all things of the world and wake up and stimulate in us the capacity of the Love. They contribute to balance.

ARCHANGELS: They make it possible to unify our material and spiritual world. They help us to distinguish the good from the evil and access to the knowledge the Universe provides us.

ANGELS: They support us on the way to realization. They reveal us the secret aspects our being, our gifts and our repressions, and they are closest to humankind in heavenly proximity and due to that closeness, they are nearest to us in they physicality of being our couriers through life and death.

CHAPTER THIRTEEN

How Work with Angel Technology

There are 72 angels, each name a manifestation of
God's virtues. Each rule attributes and times.
Utilize the charts to ascertain your own particular
guardians.

For each angel I will write the Hebrew translation
and if you study Hebrew and it's deep
numerological and mystical meanings you will
derive even greater meaning from your angels and
all angels in particular.

It is also important to add, all angels are available to
you for their particular attribute. You need only
contact that Angel to invoke the attribute.
However, your particular three hold specific
meaning in your emotional, spiritual and physical
attributes and should be acknowledged each and
every day if possible.

In this book, I will arrange them chronologically
and by month and then and describe the attributes of
each Angel governing that month.

The most important thing to remember is they must
not be worshipped, only God can be worshipped,
Angels are messengers and guardians for times
when we are in need of comfort.

For me Angels came when I most confused and
most clear. My life was beginning to shape itself of
it's own will, of course through my past
experiences, but also as it began to fill out,
especially my career, my need for love was last to
be fulfilled and for various reasons, I would have to
live without love while I mended. I had love of my
family, that sustained by lack of romantic love. Not
that I didn't love people, but I was unavailable to
give it for my own reasons, not especially
important. But important enough that I knew I
needed strength over the next few months to survive
my loneliness and deep need. I thought I would get
to the end of that tunnel, but some days and nights
were too unbearable and I thought I would break.

This lead me to deep spiritual searches which led
me. Our fight for our souls and the souls of our

human planet. The Angels of light fight against the fallen Angels and every religion professes this.

I also knew in many instances I felt no one person could feel my pain or understand and I had no desire to open up myself to anyone either. I knew my relationship with the creator and with the creator's angels was one of unconditional love and I was looking for the miracle of redemption, comfort and support. My angels would never forsake me, judge me and were forever present. With this knowledge I could walk the Earth through, racism, bigotry, hate, ignorance and loneliness.

With the utterance of my Angel prayers to God, I knew I could live one more day, survive one more night, make a miracle. I also felt because of the persecution as people of color so many of us feel Angels and the Creator were the one source that meant, even if you never knew a father, a mother, a mentor they were there for you in the most purest sense, yourself. And the attributes you were born with were God given and no one could claim them or disclaim, they are yours from your first to last breath. And that was a comfort of the deepest level.

I hear so often, the lack of role models in our community, well you know what in the world of the Creator and Angels you are your own role model, the Creator is your commander in chief, the Angels the army just for you.

And as we experience life the good, the bad, the ugly and the beautiful, trust and faith in a higher Power, God, understand God's will be done and if you're like me, I believe each and every soul is put here to learn and progress. Whatever your limited or expanded learning may be it's to create a soul worthy of compassion and intelligence and someone who sees beyond the physical matter in this Universe. Whatever happens to you, trust, whether you might die tomorrow, live another day, you are approaching a moment of truth and if you are reading this book, you've already decided there's more to this world than meets the eye and you want to know more. And knowing more is that key to never ending glory.

The following tables are of the 72 guardian angels are derived from Exodus 14, versus 19, 20 and 21.

Each are an aspect God, manifested in many of the Angel names by the "el" or "al" at the end of each name. This list is in direct correlation to the hebrew configuration of the miracle of the parting of the Red Sea. On a deeper level it is a code which unlocks miracles. I will describe the particular aspect of each angel. This list is also linked to times of birth and the Angel who "rules" that period of time. Each Angel is a block of 20 minutes in 24 hour day. These Angels can also be re-listed according to month and day of birth.

In terms of Angel influences and the days they rule, the corresponding charts locate those times and days. On the Physical Angel Chart, the listed Angel is in influence, On the Emotional Chart , the Angel Rules over those days, Finally, on the Spiritual Angel chart, those are the times the listed Angel in is prioritized influence.

This is the double, triple, several duty assignments of Angels. The act of being specific is helpful, but not imperative. It is the attribute of the Angel that you would most want to invoke for your purposes. It takes deeper attention to be able to be specific on day, month and hour—but we are in the higher learning realms where observance and understanding of the basic technology is key. With study and time we become better versed micro specifics, but we must deal in the macro specifics first.

CHAPTER FOURTEEN

ANGEL DIAGRAMS

HOW TO FIND YOUR PHYSICAL ANGEL

Find your date of birth in this table and find your Physical Guardian Angel.

JANUARY	FEBRUARY	MARCH
NEMAMIAH : 1 to January 3 IEIALEL : 4 to January 8 HARAHEL : 9 to January 13 MITZRAEL : 14 to January 18 UMABEL : 19 to January 23 IAH-HEL : 24 to January 28 ANAUEL : 29 to January 31	ANAUEL : 1 to February 2 MEHIEL : 3 to February 7 DAMABIAH : 8 to February 12 MANAKEL : 13 to February 17 EIAEL : 18 to February 22 HABUHIAH : 23 to February 28 ROCHEL : February 29	ROCHEL : 1 to March 4 JABAMIAH : 5 to March 9 HAIAIEL : 10 to March 14 MUMIAH : 15 to March 19 VEHUIAH : 20 to March 24 JELIEL : 25 to March 29 SITAEL : 30 to March 31

APRIL	MAY	JUNE
SITAEL : 1 to April 3 ELEMIAH : 4 to April 8 MAHASIAH : 9 to April 13 LELAHEL : 14 to April 18 ACHAIAH : 19 to April 23 CAHETHEL : 24 to April 29 HAZIEL : April 30	HAZIEL : 1 to May 4 ALADIAH : 5 to May 9 LAUVUEL : 10 to May 14 HAHAIAH : 15 to May 19 IEZALEL : 20 to May 24 MEBAHEL : 25 to May 29 HARIEL : 30 to May 31	HARIEL : 1 to June 3 HAKAMIAH : 4 to June 8 LAUVIAH : 9 to June 13 CALIEL : 14 to June 19 LEUVIAH : 20 to June 24 PAHALIAH : 25 to June 30

JULY	AUGUST	SEPTEMBER
NELCHAEL : 1 to July 5 IEIAIEL : 6 to July 10 MELAHEL : 11 to July 15 HAHIUIAH : 16 to July 20 NITH-HAIAH : 21 to July 25 HAAIAH : 26 to July 31	IERATHEL : 1 to August 5 SEHEIAH : 6 to August 10 REIIEL : 11 to August 15 OMAEL : 16 to August 20 LECABEL : 21 to August 25 VASARIAH : 26 to August 31	IEHUIAH : 1 to September 5 LEHAHIAH : 6 to September 10 CHAVAKIAH : 11 to the 15 seven. MENADEL : 16 to the 20 seven. ANIEL : 21 to September 25 HAAMIAH : 26 to the 30 seven.
OCTOBER	**NOVEMBER**	**DECEMBER**
REHAEL : 1 to October 5 IEIAZEL : 6 to October 10 HAHAHEL : 11 to October 15 MIKAEL : 16 to October 20 VEUALIAH : 21 to October 25 IELAHAIAH : 26 to October 30 SEALIAH : October 31	SEALIAH : 1 to November 4 ARIEL : 5 to November 9 ASALIAH : 10 to November 14 MIHAEL : 15 to November 19 VEHUEL : 20 to November 24 DANIEL : 25 to November 29 HAHASIAH : November 30	HAHASIAH : 1 to December 4 IMAMIAH : 5 to December 9 NANAEL : 10 to December 14 NITHAEL : 15 to December 19 MEBAIAH : 20 to December 24 POIEL : 25 to December 29 NEMAMIAH : 30 to the 31 déc.

CHART 2 HOW TO FIND YOUR EMOTIONAL ANGEL

VEHUIAH March 20, May 31, August 11, October 22, January 2, March 14	JELIEL March 21, 1er June, August 12, October 23, January 3, March 15	SITAEL March 22, June 2, August 13, October 24, January 4, March 16
ELEMIAH March 23, June 3, August 14, October 25, January 5, March 17	MAHASIAH March 24, June 4, August 15, October 26, January 6, March 18	LELAHEL March 25, June 5, August 16, October 27, January 7, March 19
ACHAIAH March 26, June 6, August 17, October 28, January 8	CAHETHEL March 27, June 7, August 18, October 29, January 9	HAZIEL March 28, June 8, August 19, October 30, January 10
ALADIAH March 29, June 9, August 20, October 31, January 11	LAUVUEL March 30, June 10, August 21, 1er November, January 12	HAHAIAH March 31, June 11, August 22, November 2, January 13
IEZALEL 1er April, June 12, August 23, November 3, January 14	MEBAHEL April 2, June 13, August 24, November 4, January 15	HARIEL April 3, June 14, August 25, November 5, January 16
HAKAMIAH April 4, June 15, August 26, November 6, January 17	LAUVIAH April 5, June 16, August 27, November 7, January 18	CALIEL April 6, June 17, August 28, November 8, January 19

LEUVIAH April 7, June 18, August 29, November 9, January 20	**PAHALIAH** April 8, June 19, August 30, November 10, January 21	**NELCHAEL** April 9, June 20, August 31, November 11, January 22
IEIAIEL April 10, June 21, 1er September, November 12, January 23	**MELAHEL** April 11, June 22, September 2, November 13, January 24	**HAHIUIAH** April 12, June 23, September 3, November 14, January 25
NITH-HAIAH April 13, June 24, September 4, November 15, January 26	**HAAIAH** April 14, June 25, September 5, November 16, January 27	**IERATHEL** April 15, June 26, September 6, November 17, January 28
SEHEIAH April 16, June 27, September 7, November 18, January 29	**REIIEL** April 17, June 28, September 8, November 19, January 30	**OMAEL** April 18, June 29, September 9, November 20, January 31,
LECABEL April 19, June 30, September 10, November 21, 1er February	**VASARIAH** April 20, 1er July, September 11, November 22, February 2	**IEHUIAH** April 21, July 2, September 12, November 23, February 3
LEHAHIAH April 22, July 3, September 13, November 24, February 4	**CHAVAKIAH** April 23, July 4, September 14, November 25, February 5	**MENADEL** April 24, July 5, September 15, November 26, February 6
ANIEL April 25, July 6, September 16, November 27, February 7	**HAAMIAH** April 26, July 7, September 17, November 28, February 8	**REHAEL** April 27, July 8, September 18, November 29, February 9

IEIAZEL	HAHAHEL	MIKAEL
April 28, July 9, September 19, November 30, February 10	April 29, July 10, September 20, 1er December, February 11	April 30, July 11, September 21, December 2, February 12
VEUALIAH	IELAHAIAH	SEALIAH
1er May, July 12, September 22, December 3, February 13	May 2, July 13, September 23, December 4, February 14	May 3, July 14, September 24, December 5, February 15
ARIEL	ASALIAH	MIHAEL
May 4, July 15, September 25, December 6, February 16	May 5, July 16, September 26, December 7, February 17	May 6, July 17, September 27, December 8, February 18
VEHUEL	DANIEL	HAHASIAH
May 7, July 18, September 28, December 9, February 19	May 8, July 19, September 29, December 10, February 20	May 9, July 20, September 30, December 11, February 21
IMAMIAH	NANAEL	NITHAEL
May 10, July 21, 1er October, December 12, February 22	May 11, July 22, October 2, December 13, February 23	May 12, July 23, October 3, December 14, February 24
MEBAIAH	POIEL	NEMAMIAH
May 13, July 24, October 4, December 15, February 25	May 14, July 25, October 5, December 16, February 26	May 15, July 26, October 6, December 17, February 27

IEIALEL May 16, July 27, October 7, December 18, February 28	**HARAHEL** May 17, July 28, October 8, December 19, February 29	**MITZRAEL** May 18, July 29, October 9, December 20, 1er March
UMABEL May 19, July 30, October 10, December 21, March 2	**IAH-HEL** May 20, July 31, October 11, December 22, March 3	**ANAUEL** May 21, 1er August, October 12, December 23, March 4
MEHIEL May 22, August 2, October 13, December 24, March 5	**DAMABIAH** May 23, August 3, October 14, December 25, March 6	**MANAKEL** May 24, August 4, October 15, December 26, March 7
EIAEL May 25, August 5, October 16, December 27, March 8	**HABUHIAH** May 26, August 6, October 17, December 28, March 9	**ROCHEL** May 27, August 7, October 18, December 29, March 10
JABAMIAH May 28, August 8, October 19, December 30, March 11	**HAIAIEL** May 29, August 9, October 20, December 31, March 12	**MUMIAH** May 30, August 10, October 21, 1er January, March 13

CHART 3 HOW TO FIND YOUR SPIRITUAL ANGEL
according to the time and place you where born and
converted to Greenwich Mean Time

ANGELS	HOURS	ANGELS	HOURS
VEHUIAH	0h to 0h20	ANIEL	12h to 12h20
JELIEL	0h20 to 0h40	HAAMIAH	12h20 to 12h40
SITAEL	0h40 to 1h	REHAEL	12h40 to 13h
ELEMIAH	1h to 1h20	IEIAZEL	13h to 13h20
MAHASIAH	1h20 to 1h40	HAHAHEL	13h20 to 13h40
LELAHEL	1h40 to 2h	MIKAEL	13h40 to 14h
ACHAIAH	2h to 2h20	VEUALIAH	14h to 14h20
CAHETHEL	2h20 to 2h40	IELAHAIAH	14h20 to 14h40
HAZIEL	2h40 to 3h	SEALIAH	14h40 to 15h
ALADIAH	3h to 3h20	ARIEL	15h to 15h20
LAUVUEL	3h20 to 3h40	ASALIAH	15h20 to 15h40
HAHAIAH	3h40 to 4h	MIHAEL	15h40 to 16h
IEZALEL	4h to 4h20	VEHUEL	16h to 16h20
MEBAHEL	4h20 to 4h40	DANIEL	16h20 to 16h40
HARIEL	4h40 to 5h	HAHASIAH	16h40 to 17h
HAKAMIAH	5h to 5h20	IMAMIAH	17h to 17h20
LAUVIAH	5h20 to 5h40	NANAEL	17h20 to 17h40

CALIEL	5h40 to 6h	NITHAEL	17h40 to 18h
LEUVIAH	6h to 6h20	MEBAIAH	18h to 18h20
PAHALIAH	6h20 to 6h40	POIEL	18h20 to 18h40
NELCHAEL	6h40 to 7h	NEMAMIAH	18h40 to 19h
IEIAIEL	7h to 7h20	IEIALEL	19h to 19h20
MELAHEL	7h20 to 7h40	HARAHEL	19h20 to 19h40
HAHIUIAH	7h40 to 8h	MITZRAEL	19h40 to 20h
NITH-HAIAH	8h to 8h20	UMABEL	20h to 20h20
HAAIAH	8h20 to 8h40	IAH-HEL	20h20 to 20h40
IERATHEL	8h40 to 9h	ANAUEL	20h40 to 21h
SEHEIAH	9h to 9h20	MEHIEL	21h to 21h20
REIIEL	9h20 to 9h40	DAMABIAH	21h20 to 21h40
OMAEL	9h40 to 10h	MANAKEL	21h40 to 22h
LECABEL	10h to 10h20	EIAEL	22h to 22h20
VASARIAH	10h20 to 10h40	HABUHIAH	22h20 to 22h40
IEHUIAH	10h40 to 11h	ROCHEL	22h40 to 23h
LEHAHIAH	11h to 11h20	JABAMIAH	23h to 23h20
CHAVAKIAH	11h20 to 11h40	HAIAIEL	23h20 to 23h40
MENADEL	11h40 to 12h	MUMIAH	23h40 to 24h

The Spiritual Angel chart requires reconciling the time and place of your birth with Greenwich Mean Time. (The hours between brackets are those where time changes take place. When no hour is indicated, the change is done at midnight.) These calculations are using time zones in France, so a bit of math is required. Since 1945, France was aligned on the meridian line of Central Europe and thus there is one hour less variation in all the years between the solar hour and standard time. It is thus necessary to reconcile the hour of your birth by subtracting the number of hours indicated in this table. H/h equals hour. REMEMBER WE ARE USING THE 24 HOUR CLOCK.

Before 1916, standard time = solar hour		
	Winter	Summer
01/01/1916 to the 25/02/1940[2h]	0 H	- 1 H
25/02/1940[2h] to the 09/05/1940	- 1 H	
	Free zone	Occupied zone
10/05/1940 to the 04/05/1941	- 1 H	- 2 H
05/05/1941 to the 06/10/1941	- 2 H	- 2 H
07/10/1941 to the 08/03/1942	- 1 H	- 2 H
09/03/1942 to the 02/11/1942[3h]	- 2 H	- 2 H
02/11/1942[3h] to the 29/03/1943[2h]	- 1 H	
29/03/1943[2h] to the 04/10/1943[3h]	- 2 H	
04/10/1943[3h] to the 03/04/1944[2h]	- 1 H	
03/04/1944[2h] to the 08/10/1944[1h]	- 2 H	
08/10/1944[1h] to the 02/04/1945[2h]	- 1 H	
02/04/1945[2h] to the 16/09/1945[3h]	- 2 H	
16/09/1945[3h] to the 28/03/1976[1h]	- 1 H	
	Winter	Summer
since the 28/03/1976[1h]	- 1h	- 2 H

Calculation:

GMT convert to your time zone then -1

So, in meteorology for the Northern hemisphere: spring begins
on 1 March, summer on 1 June, autumn on 1 September, and
winter on 1 December

Some facts about how TIME is measured

Greenwich Mean Time also prime meridian

The zero meridian (0°), used as a reference line
from which longitude east and west is measured. It
passes through Greenwich, England.

PURPOSE AND BENEFIT OF STUDY OF NAMES OF G-D/NAMES OF CORRELATED ANGELS

This is the function to Torah *[i.e. study of Old Testament, Prophets/Writings, Biblical Law, particularly by reading it in ancient texts of Aramaic and Hebrew due to hypertext PARDES component]*: **to introduce a unity of purpose to the diverse objects, forces and peoples of creation, uniting them all in the harmonious endeavor of serving the divine objective in creation.**

(The Chassidic Masters)
Source: chabaddotorg

CHAPTER FIFTEEN

WHICH ANGEL TO MEDITATE TO FOR A PARTICULAR NEED

Abstract sciences, influences   Hahasiah

Accidents, protects against	Anianuel
Accusations, aids against false, unjust	Vasariah
Adversity, helps and consoles in	Etaiel
Adversity, helps and protects against	Sitael
Adversity, protects against,	Hahaiah
Agricultural produce, dominates	Cahetel
Agriculture, governs	Xabuiah
Ambassadors, influences	Haaiah
Anger, calms	Manakel
Animals, dominates the creation (origination) of	Omael
Animals, protects against fierce	Mehiel
Archives, rules	Harakel
Arrogant and proud, helps defeat the	Sealiah
Arsenal, dominates	Hakamiah
Artists, influences	Ieiazel
Arts, governs	Aniel
Arts, influences	Hariel
Asking, serves to obtain what is asked for	Poiel
Astrology, influences	Lecabel
Astronomy, dominates	Umabel
Attacks, protects against unjust	Jerathel
Believers, influences (missionaries)	Hahahel
Blessings, serves to obtain	Cahetel
Books, governs	Ieiazel
Business trips, influences	Ieialiel
Business, dominates fortune	Ieialiel
Business, influences	Anianuel
Businessmen, influences	Anianuel
Calamity, helps and protects against	Sitael
Carefulness, aids in	Seeiah
Change, dominates	Etaiel
Chastity, rules	Pahaliah
Cheerfulness, influences	Leuviah
Chemistry, dominates	Hahasiah
Children, helps those who wish to have	Mebaiah
Civilization, governs over	Jerathel
Collapse, protects against (of land and structures)	Seeiah
Combatatants, influences	Nemamiah

Consciousness, expanding	Vehuiah
Consolation, helps in	Mebaiah
Contemplation and reflection, influences	Asaliah
Conversions, aids in	Pahaliah
Countries, helps maintain peace and harmony between	Lehahiah
Courage, in battle	Ielahiah
Creeds, governs (faiths)	Haamiah
Cures contagious diseases	Lelahel
Curiosity, influences	Mikael
Defeatists, serves against	Hariel
Desperation, aids against and	Omael
Devotion, governs	Lehahiah
Difficult solutions, aids and influences	Ariel
Discoveries and new methods	Hariel
Discoveries, influences	Elemiah
Disease, cures	Xabuiah
Disease, protects and cures	Rehael
Dreams and sleep, influences	Manakel
Dreams, revelations in	Nith-haiah
Dreams, rules	Hahaiah
Dynasties, dominates (kings, princes)	Nitael
Earth, governs the	Xabuiah
Education, influences	Sealiah
Enemies, aids in confounding our	Jerathel
Enemies, aids in victory over	Hakamiah
Enemies, frees us from	Ieiazel
Enemies, helps destroy	Veuahiah
Enemies, Helps destroy	Imamiah
Enemies, protects against all (visible and invisible)	Reiiel
Energy, dominates	Imamiah
Enlightened, governs the	Iah-hel
Enlightenment, receiving	Vehuiah
Enlightenment, serves to obtain	Nanael
Envy, protects against	Mebahel
Evil, confounds the	Haiel
Evil, helps defeat the	Sealiah
Exiled, aids in return to their native land	Menadel
Exiled, governs the	Hahuiah

Eye, heals diseases of the	Leialel
Faith, dominates good	Aziel
Faith, influences	Aziel
Faithfulness and piety, governs	Mebaiah
Faithfulness, aids in conjugal	Iezalel
Faithfulness, governs	Lehahiah
Faithfulness, influences	Mizrael
Fame, dominates	Lauviah
Fame, dominates	Lelahel
Fame, influences	Rochel
Fame, rules	Poiel
Famous, influences the learned who become	Lauviah
Fatherly love, influences	Rehael
Fears, conquer	Menadel
Female sterility, protects against	Harakel
Fertility, dominates	Xabuiah
Fighters, influences	Nemamiah
Fire, protects against	Seeiah
Fisherman, governs	Namabiah
Fortune in business, dominates	Ieialiel
Fortune, dominates	Lelahel
Fortune, influences	Poiel
Fortune, protects against those who envy your	Mebahel
Frankness, influences	Hakamiah
Freedom from slavery	Veuahiah
Friendship of the great, obtain the.	Aziel
Friendship, dominates	Iezalel
Friendship, helps recover of those we've offended	Chevakiah
Friendship, serves to obtain the (of a person)	Umabel
Generals, dominates	Nemamiah
Generations and origination, dominates	Michael
Generous spirit, dominates magnanimity	Sitael
Geometry, dominates	Nelehael
Grace, protects and aids in obtaining	Leuviah
Grace, serves to obtain	Hahuiah
Happy conclusion, brings every experience to a	Mumiah
Harmony and union between spouses, helps preserve	Michael
Harmony, leads to inner	Jabamiah

Healing, Influences	Aladiah
Health and healing, maintains	Anianuel
Health and longevity, dominates	Rehael
Health and longevity, governs	Seeiah
Heart, influences sensitivity of the	Umabel
Helps maintain health and	Xabuiah
Hide that which one does wish to reaveal	Aladiah
Humankind, influences all	Jeliel
Humility, influences	Vehuel
Hunting, influences	Cahetel
Industry, influences	Achaiah
Infernal spirits, protects	Haamiah
Innocence, aids in the triumph of	Caliel
Inspires in decision-making	Daniel
Intelligence, influences	Leuviah
Iron, influences	Haiel
Iron, influences	Leialel
Irreverent, Helps against	Hahahel
Joviality, influences	Leuviah
Judges, dominates	Rochel
Judges, governs	Vasariah
Judges, influences	Daniel
Judicial, dominates the system	Caliel
Justice, dominates	Mebahel
Justice, dominates	Asaliah
Justice, dominates	Daniel
Justice, governs	Vasariah
Kings and princes, Rules	Jeliel
Knowledge, helps obtain	Iah-hel
Law, men of (influences)	Nanael
Laws, dominates	Rochel
Lawsuits, protects and helps win a	Ielahiah
Learning, influences	Mahasiah
Leprosy, protects against and heals	Manakel
Light on our jobs (occupations), serves to cast	Lecabel
Light, influences the spread	Achaiah
Light, protects those who seek true	Haaiah
Light, serves to acquire	Lelahel

Peace, dominates	Veuahiah
Peace, Helps to live in witheveryone	Mahasiah
Peace, influences	Jerathel
Persecutors, release from	Mizrael
Personalities, dominates great	Vehuel
Philosophers, governs	Iah-hel
Philosophical knowledge, dominates	Jabamiah
Philosophy, dominates	Reiiel
Physics, dominates	Umabel
Plague, Rules over	Aladiah
Plots, serves to uncover and undo plans	Iehuiah
Poets, influences	Lauviah
Politics, influences	Mikael
Powerful, dominates the	Mikael
Prelates, governs	Hahahel
Press and books, influences the	Mehiel
Press, dominates the and	Ieiazel
Press, influences the	Harakel
Priests, governs	Hahahel
Prisoners, aids in the release of	Menadel
Prisoners, helps prosper and release	Nemamiah
Prisoners, helps release	Ieiazel
Prisoners, protects	Imamiah
Promises, helps keep	Aziel
Prosperity, influences	Veuahiah
Protection against evil spirits.	Cahetel
Protects and consoles	Daniel
Prudence, governs	Seeiah
Rabies, protects against	Mehiel
Rabies, Rules over	Aladiah
Rebellious children, protects against	Harakel
Reconciliation, aids and	Iezalel
Regenerates and protects	Jabamiah
Release from enemies, grants	Haiel
Religion, governs	Mebaiah
Religion, influences	Pahaliah
Research, influences	Imamiah
Respect, governs	Lehahiah

Reveals traitors	Elemiah
Revelations in dreams	Nith-haiah
Revitalizing, during the night	Lauviah
Revolts, helps repress unjust	Jeliel
Ruin, protects against (of land and structures)	Seeiah
Rulers, influences just (honorable)	Iehuiah
Sacred, governs all people and things	Reiiel
Sadness, aids against	Lauviah
Safety, Helps and protects in journeys	Mikael
Sailors, influences	Namabiah
Schorlarly and learned, influences	Mehiel
Sciences, dominates the high	Lauviah
Sciences, dominates the higher	Nanael
Sciences, dominates	Hariel
Sciences, dominates	Vehuiah
Sciences, governs	Aniel
Sciences, influences	Lelahel
Sciences, influences abstract	Hahasiah
Sea voyages, dominates	Elemiah
Secrets, discovering natural	Achaiah
Secrets, keeping	Aladiah
Sharing, influences friendly	Chevakiah
Shipwrecks, protects against	Ieialiel
Shrewd, influences the	Vehuiah
Shrewdness, influences	Iezalel
Siege, helps conquer and obtain release from.	Aniel
Sincerity, influences	Aziel
Slander, protects against	Menadel
Slanderers, aids against	Hahahel
Slanderers, protects against	Nelehael
Sleep and dreams, influences	Manakel
Sociability, dominates	Iezalel
Soldiers, dominates	Haiel
Soldiers, influences	Nemamiah
Solitude, influences virtue in	Iah-hel
Sorcery, aids against	Namabiah
Spirit, governs	Chevakiah
Spirit, helps heal the ills of the	Mizrael

Spirit, the last	Mumiah
Spirits unfavorable, protects against	Nelehael
Spiritual people, influences	Hahaiah
Spiritual torment, aids against	Elemiah
Spirituality, helps those who wish to raise their	Asaliah
Stability, governs	Nitael
Sterility, protects against female	Harakel
children, protect against rebellious	Harakel
Stolen or lost objects, helps find	Rochel
Storms, protects against	Ieialiel
Success, dominates	Poiel
Supernatural and occult sciences, influences	Etaiel
Supernatural magic, dominates	Mahasiah
Supernatural mysteries, helps those who wish to know	Hahasiah
Supernatural sciences, governs	Nith-haiah
Teachers, influences	Nanael
Theology, dominates	Pahaliah
Theology, influences	Mahasiah
Thieves, protects against	Hahuiah
Trade, dominates	Anianuel
Traitors, aids against and	Hakamiah
Traitors, serves to uncover	Iehuiah
Travel, protects against dangers of	Melahel
Treasures, dominates	Harakel
Treasures, helps rediscover hidden	Ariel
Trials, influences	Caliel
Trouble, aids against	Omael
Trouble, helps against	Leialel
Trouble, helps find peace against	Vehuel
Truth known, serves to make the	Caliel
Truth, influences and protects	Mebahel
Truth, influences lovers of	Sitael
Truth, protects all those who seek	Haaiah
Truth, protects and influences those who seek	Haamiah
Unspiritual, serves against the	Hariel
Vegetation, dominates	Lecabel
Vegetation, dominates	Manakel
Vegitation, dominates	Sealiah

Victory, dominates	Ielahiah
Victory, grants	Haiel
Victory, obtaining	Lauviah
Virtue, dominates men of	Mizrael
Warriors, influences	Nemamiah
Water, rules over	Melahel
Waters, dominates the	Namabiah
Weapons, dominates	Haiel
Weapons, protects against	Melahel
Will, influences influences	Chevakiah
Wisdom, aids to obtain	Namabiah
Wisdom, helps obtain and	Iah-hel
Wisdom, obtain	Etaiel
Wisdom, serves to obtain	Nith-haiah
Wise, influences meditation of the	Aniel
Wise, influences the	Hahaiah
Wise, presides over the	Nith-haiah
Witnesses, influences	Caliel
Words, influences	Vasariah

CHAPTER SIXTEEN

Angel Numerology

Number Sequences From G-d and Angels

through a third-born (Moses, the third child of
Amram and Jocheved) on the third day in the third
month.
(Talmud, Shabbat 88a)
The Torah is associated with the number "3"
because the ultimate function
of Torah is "to make peace in the world" and "3"
represents the
concept of peace.
Peace is unity in diversity. The number "1" implies
exclusivity and singularity;
the number "2" connotes diversity and plurality; the
number
"3" represents a state in which the diversity of "2"
is superceded by a
third, encompassing truth, within whose context
differences no longer

divide but rather unite diverse components into a
harmonious whole.
Source: Chabaddotorg

Your angels often communicate messages to you by
showing you sequences of numbers. They do this in
two ways. First, they subtly whisper in your ear so
you'll look up in time to notice the clock's time or a
phone number on a billboard. The angels hope
you'll be aware that you're seeing this same number
sequence repeatedly. For instance, you may
frequently see the number sequence 111, and it
seems every time you look at a clock the time reads
1:11 or 11:11.
The second way in which angels show you
meaningful number sequences is by physically
arranging for, say, a car to drive in front of you that
has a specific license plate number they want you to
see. Those who are aware of this phenomenon
become adept at reading the meaning of various
license plates. In this way, the angels will actually
give you detailed messages. Here are the basic
meanings of various number sequences. However,
your own angels will tell you if your situation holds
a different meaning for you. Ask your angels,

"What are you trying to tell me?" and they'll happily give you additional information to help decode their numeric meanings.

The angels do their best to get our attention and to communicate with us. In this way, they help us heal our own lives. However, we often discount the signs they give us, writing them off as mere coincidences or our imagination. The angels say: "We can't write our messages to you in the sky. You've got to pay attention and believe when you see any patterns forming in your life - especially in response to any questions or prayers you've posed. When you hear the same song repeatedly or see the same number sequence, who do you think is behind this? Your angels, of course!"

Power Numbers

111 - Monitor your thoughts carefully, and be sure to only think about what you want, not what you don't want. This sequence is a sign that there is a gate of opportunity opening up, and your thoughts are manifesting into form at record speeds. The 111

is like the bright light of a flash bulb. It means the universe has just taken a snapshot of your thoughts and is manifesting them into form. Are you pleased with what thoughts the universe has captured? If not, correct your thoughts (ask your angels to help you with this if you have difficulty controlling or monitoring your thoughts).

222 - Our newly planted ideas are beginning to grow into reality. Keep watering and nurturing them, and soon they will push through the soil so you can see evidence of your manifestation. In other words, don't quit five minutes before the miracle. Your manifestation is soon going to be evident to you, so keep up the good work! Keep holding positive thoughts, keep affirming, and continue visualizing.

333 - The Ascended Masters are near you, desiring you to know that you have their help, love, and companionship. Call upon the Ascended Masters often, especially when you see the number 3 patterns around you. Some of the more famous Ascended Masters include: Jesus, Moses, Mary, Quan Yin, and Yogananda.

444 - The angels are surrounding you now, reassuring you of their love and help. Don't worry because the angels' help is nearby.

555 - Buckle your seatbelts. A major life change is upon you. This change should not be viewed as being "positive" or "negative," since all change is but a natural part of life's flow. Perhaps this change is an answer to your prayers, so continue seeing and feeling yourself being at peace.

666 - Your thoughts are out of balance right now, focused too much on the material world. This number sequence asks you to balance your thoughts between heaven and earth. Like the famous "Sermon on the Mount," the angels ask you to focus on spirit and service, and know your material and emotional needs will automatically be met as a result.

777 - The angels applaud you…congratulations, you're on a roll! Keep up the good work and know your wish is coming true. This is an extremely positive sign and means you should also expect more miracles to occur.

888 - A phase of your life is about to end, and this is a sign to give you forewarning to prepare. This number sequence may mean you are winding up an

emotional career, or relationship phase. It also means there is light at the end of the tunnel. In addition, it means, "The crops are ripe. Don't wait to pick and enjoy them." In other words, don't procrastinate making your move or enjoying fruits of your labor.

999 - Completion. This is the end of a big phase in your personal or global life. Also, it is a message to lightworkers involved in Earth healing and means, "Get to work because Mother Earth needs you right now."

000 - A reminder you are one with God, and to feel the presence of your Creator's love within you. Also, it is a sign that a situation has gone full circle.

Since Pope Gregory the Great (604 AD), the teaching of the Nine Choirs of Angels has been accepted in the Roman Catholic Church.

The following are a list of the Hebrew names for the above: these could also be the names of **seventy-two angels** of **Jacob's ladder**, or the **seventy-two syllable name of God**, made up of **216 letters**.

Also the 360 degree grand circle of the Mazzaroth is 25,920 years divided by 72 names is 360 years per each of God's names to manifest itself in the world. One zodiacal age is 2160 years containing six 360 year periods.

- Knowledge of the Word of God, and ruling ones life according to the word of God.

The 72 angels bearing the mystical name of god - There are three verses in exodus (as stated earlier) each containing seventy-two letters. By writing down the first of these, and underneath this the next verse backward, and under this again the last verse forwards, 72 columns of three letters each are obtained.these are read downwards, and the terminations "al" or "ah", according as they are male or female, appended. There is also an attribution of these intelligences, one to each of the quinaries or segments of five degrees of the zodiac; but there are also innumerable other angels, demons, magical images, lords of triplicities, lesser assistant angels and so on , with demons to correspond. It is well to bear in mind that all angels whatever their state of grace , indeed, no matter how christologically corrupt and defiant - are under god, even when, to all intents and purposes,they are performing under the direct orders of the devil. Evil itself is an instrumentality of the creator, who uses evil for his own divine ,if unsearchable,ends. Angels perform a multiplicity of duties and tasks. Preeminently they serve god. They also carry out missions from god to man. But many serve man directly asguardians, counselors ,guides,judges, interpreters, cooks, comforters, match- makers and gravediggers.

Metratonic Numbers

I am [state your name 3 times] - [Example: "I
am Bob. I am Bob. I am Bob."}
I open this portal of [place the digital code here.
Example 11:11] and I bring the energies of the
[repeat the digital code] into my heart.
I expand them. [Repeat this 3 times].
I will use these energies for my highest good
and for the highest good concerned.
I will create
I will manifest
I desire
Now state your wish. NEVER use the words
WANT or NEED.
I now release these energies to the ethers.
So be it.
So it is.

What are angels? To me, an angel is an archetypal
image of a good thought. In other words, instead of
sending a good thought to someone, one can send a
PICTURE of a good thought - an angel. The word
malach - ANGEL means MESSENGER.
It is possible to prove to yourself whether there are
angels, and if so, if they will work in your life. No

one need know that you are doing this, so if it does not work, you will not look foolish. Simply picture an angel in your head and send it to someone that you are worried about, or angry with, or someone that you are worried about, or angry with, or someone in pain. And then watch to see if it makes a difference. The results may surprise you.

ANGELS AND NUMBERS

We look at the clocks on our microwaves, autos, and watches. Over and over again we see 11:11, 12:12, 1:11 2:22 etc. We innately know that these numerical digits are important but cannot seem to find the data that will explain the phenomena. Our eyes feel the frequency of completion as we enter into the remembering of each optical mantra.

When you experience the numerical downloads whether MASTER NUMBERS (all the same numbers) or PERSONAL CODES (seeing the same mixed numbers over and over again) stop for one full minute, allowing this energy to be birthed through you. Focus on your deepest desire and see it as manifest. The universe has just taken a picture of your thoughts. Empty yourself of any preconceived notions and let the light sew up the frayed edges of your intentions. Each and every number within your personal universe is triggering your subconscious into a new pattern of DNA configurations.

POWER NUMBERS

111...Energy flow. Enhancing whatever level you are in presently. The Date Nov 11 is a very strong time Known as 11:11 A time for Change and Awakening...

222...Resurrection and ascension process.

333...Decision number. Either directs you into a phase of 999 completion, or negativity, it puts you in the 666 frequency which throws you back into the third dimension.

444...This is an actual resurrection number.

You have just completed an important phase.

555...Experiencing the energy or a level of Christ Consciousness, very significant.

666...Material World. Third dimensional frequency. Denseness.

777...Symbolized an integration of some portion of the four lower bodies with higher spiritual frequencies within the third dimensional plane, or at the level in which you are manifesting your physical reality on the Earth Plane.

888...Symbolized infinity. The unified spiral of the physical merging with the spiritual. Moving toward the completion of the ascension
process through the energies of the 222 and 444.

999...Symbolized the three levels of the triune. Completion.

000...Great Void. Experiencing a Null Zone. Switching or moving into a new energy field.

11:11...Beginning of a whole new level or phase of development. Another dimension or frequency of experience. A portal way opening.

12:12...A cosmic connection. A bridge to the future. Signifies a level of completion or graduation.

RECEIVING ENERGY FROM NUMBERS

Excerpt from Gillian MacBeth-Louthan

Numbers and humans go hand in hand. From the beginning of time known we have been defined by a numerical equation whether age, birth date, weight, or the numbers of camels we have in out dowry,

numbers have always seemed to be our silent
partners.
Nowadays when a child is born the fist thing they
are given is a number that will follow them for the
rest of their lives until death at which time they will
be given a new number to define them. The
numbers on our clocks tell us when to go, when to
stop when to drink coffee, when to sleep. Numbers
are as much a part of us as our flesh.

In 1991/1992 the number 11:11 was issued to
humanity as an activation number. Escorting us
energetically into a new octave of Solar Light.
Creating a numerical signature that follows us to
this day. This past month we experienced the
number of 8:8, which allowed us to walk into
ancient Egyptian/Atlantean memories. Thus
creating a doorway in which we could understand
more of our innate self.

'000' is a reminder you are always one with the
universe. Feel yourself within the center embraced
by the Creator as you are held and love

unconditionally. Walk around the inner circle of self-completing what needs to be completed.

'11,111,11:11' is a doorway or gateway into your highest potential as a human seeking divine memory. One is a singularity within 'all that is'. The 'one' seeks itself through mirror like reflection of the world around it. This doorway offers an opportunity to surpass any limitations you have unknowingly set for yourself. One to one to one enter the oneness hidden deep within your being at the center point of your soul. This energy stays activated until 2011.

'22, 222, 22:22' is the sequence of manifestation minus the frustration. Keep a holding pattern with your intent, knowing that what you have planted by your words, deeds and actions will grow and bloom in accordance with the heavenly seasons.

'33, 333, 33:33' the holy trinity is activated within the tetrahedron (3 sided pyramid) within your DNA structure. This number offers an opportunity to connect with higher evolved spiritual beings/masters/angels/Christ whenever you view it.

'44, 444, 44:44' a foundation of light is being cemented for you. New opportunity comes without being asked. Stay balanced in what you know to be divine truth and the platform of light will solidify.

'55, 555, 55:55' the universe is making changes for you whether you ask for it or not. Allow the currents to take you into a new future full of possibilities still hidden from you at this point of seeing. Hold the vision until you land on the new shore.

Everything on earth is defined by a numerical configuration. All life can be reduced and explained by numbers. The currents of these numerical sequences bring into alignment a series of new understandings that will help to adjust and balance every human. The numbers on all levels align the body so it will be able to handle the higher definitions of photon light that is making itself known. Each number infusion is personalized to fit the needs of each individual. Allowing them the necessary ratio of light particles to numerical particles. As the brain adjusts to these new energies a lifting occurs allowing the individual to exit the human/animal ratio and be lifted into the human/light equation.

GLOSSARY OF TERMS

Ain Sof: "Without End." In Kabbalah, Hashem (God) the Transcendent, is called AIN. AIN means in Hebrew "No Thing", for Hashem is beyond existence. AIN is neither below nor above; nor is it in movement or stillness. There is nowhere AIN is. Hashem is Absolute Nothing. AIN SOF is the title of God who is everywhere. AIN SOF is the One to the Zero of AIN. This is the totality of what is and is not. AIN SOF is God the Immanent, the Absolute ALL. AIN SOF has no Attributes, because attributes can only be manifest within finite (limited, bounded) existence realms and AIN SOF is (Infinite, Unbounded, Limitless) and Transcendant.

G-d: When the Creator is written this way it is recognition that the name of G-d is not to be used lightly, is in some circles not to be said in it's most

Ancient Name except on the holiest of days and in very deep circle the name is unpronounceable by humankind.

<u>Who are our Guardian Angels?:</u> No evil shall befall you, nor shall affliction come near your tent, for to His Angels God has given command about you, that they guard you in all your ways. Upon their hands they will bear you up, lest you dash your foot against a stone. Psalm 91: 10-12 A heavenly spirit assigned by God to watch over each of us during our lives. The doctrine of angels is part of the Church's tradition. The role of the guardian angel is both to guide us to good thoughts, works and words, and to preserve us from evil. Since the 17th century the Church has celebrated a feast honoring them in October throughout the Universal Church. Since the last calendar revision this feast is Oct 2.

He has charged His angels with the ministry of watching and safeguarding every one of His creatures that behold not His face. Kingdoms have their angels assigned to them, and men have their angels; these latter it is to whom religion designates the Holy Guardian Angels. Our Lord says in the Gospel, "Beware lest ye scandalize any of these little ones, for their angels in heaven see the face of My Father." The existence of Guardian Angels, is, hence a dogma of the Christian faith: this being so, what ought not our respect be for that sure and holy intelligence that is ever present at our side; and how great our solicitude be, lest, by any act of ours, we offend those eyes which are ever bent upon us in all our ways.

<u>APPENDIX</u>

The basics the Hebraic Alphabet

Chart 6: The Hebrew Alphabet, their Symbolic meanings and Numerical Values
(see Glossary for deeper explanations of each letter attribute)

THE CHARACTERS AND THEIR PICTURE-IMAGES

Character		Name	Original Picture Symbolism
א		'Aleph	ox head, yoke, learn
ב		Beth	house, tent
ג		Gimel	camel's neck, soul
ד		Dáleth	door, curtain to tent
ה		He	window, lattice
ו		Wáw or váv	hook, nail, peg
ז		Zayin	weapon
ח		Cheth	hedge, fence, surround, gird
ט		Teth	serpent, snake, roll, curve
י		Yodh	hand (bent)
כ	ך	Kaph	wing, palm (hollow of the hand)
ל		Lâmedh	ox goad, correction, learning
מ	ם	Mem	waves, water
נ	ן	Nun	fish (tadpole?), snake
ס		Sâmekh	prop, support
ע		'Ayin	eye
פ	ף	Pê	mouth
צ	ץ	Tsâdhe	fish hook? tool for cutting down?
ק		Qoph	axe, monkey, back of the head
ר		Resh	head, *Boomerang quality of soul, miracles*
שׂ שׁ		Sin, Shin	tooth
ת		Tâw	sign, branded cross, mark, 'T'

#	Letter
1	Aleph
2	Beth, Veth
3	Gimel
4	Daleth
5	Heh
6	Waw
7	Zayin
8	Cheth
9	Teth
10	Jod
11	*No letter
12	*No letter
20	Kaf, Khaf
30	Lamed
40	Mem
50	Nun
60	Samech
70	Ayin
80	Peh, Pheh
90	Tzadi
100	Kof
200	Resh
300	Shin, Sin
400	Tav, Thav

THE EARTH DEGREES IN RELATION TO ANGELS

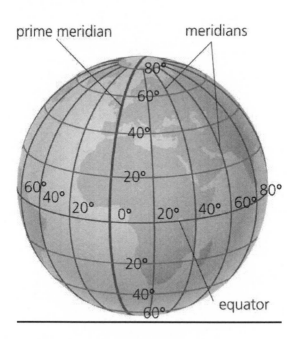

Angels Derived by the 360 Degrees of the Circle of Life=Location (Longitude, Latitude on Earth)

NAME	DEGREES IN CIRCLE	ATTRIBUTES AND INFLUENCES
Vehuiah	0 to 5	Helps receive enlightenment and to expand consciousness. Dominates the sciences and influences the shrewd.
Jeliel	6 to 10	Helps repress unjust revolts. Aids conjugal peace. Dominates kings and princes. Influences all generations.
Sitael	11 to 15	Helps and protects against adversity and calamity. Dominates magnanimity and Nobility, influences lovers of truth.
Elemiah	16 to 20	Helps against spiritual torment and reveal traitors, dominates sea voyages and the influence of discoveries.
Mahasiah	21 to 25	Helps to live in peace with everyone. Dominates supernatural magic and theology. Influences learning.

Lelahel	26 to 30	Serves to acquire "light", cure contagious diseases. Dominates love, fame and fortune. Influences the sciences.
Achaiah	31 to 35	Helps discover natural secrets. Dominates patience and restraint. Influences the spread of light and industry.
Cahetel	36 to 40	Serves to obtain blessing and protection against evil spirits. Dominates agricultural produce. Influences hunting.
Aziel	41 to 45	Helps keep promises and obtain the friendship of the great. Dominates good faith. Influences sincerity and faith.
Aladiah	46 to 50	Helps hide that which one does not wish to reveal, secrets. Dominates plague and rabies. Influences healing.
Lauviah	51 to 55	Protects against lightning and serves to obtain victory, dominates fame. Influences the learned who have become famous.
Hahaiah	56 to 60	Protects against adversity, helps when in need. Dominates dreams. Influences wise and spiritual people.
Iezalel	61 to 65	Aids reconciliation and

		conjugal faithfulness. Dominates friendship and sociability. Influences memory and shrewdness.
Mebahel	66 to 70	Protects and helps against those wishing to usurp the fortunes of others. Dominates justice. Influences and protects truth.
Hariel	71 to 75	Serves against the unspiritual and defeatists. Dominates the sciences and arts. Influences discoveries and new methods.
Hakamiah	76 to 80	Aids against traitors and victory over enemies. Dominates arsenal and influences frankness.
Lauviah	81 to 85	Aids in revitalizing during the night and against sadness. Dominates the high sciences and influences musicians and poets.
Caliel	86 to 90	Serves to make the truth known. Aids in the triumph of innocence. Dominates judicial trials and influences witnesses.
Leuviah	91 to 95	Protects and aids in obtaining grace. Dominates the memory. Influences joviality and intelligence.
Pahaliah	96 to 100	Aids in conversions. Dominates theology and religion.

Influences chastity and morals.

Nelehael	101 to 105	Protects against unfavorable spirits, against slanderers. Dominates mathematics and geometry.
Ieialiel	106 to 110	Protects against storms and shipwrecks. Dominates fortune in businesa. Influences business trips
Melahel	111 to 115	Protects against weapons and perils of travel. Dominates medicinal herbs and water.
Hahuiah	116 to 120	Serves to obtain grace. Dominates the exiled. Preserves against thieves and murderers.
Nith-haiah	121 to 125	Serves to obtain wisdom and revelations in dreams. Dominates the occult sciences and the wise.
Haaiah	126 to 130	Protects all those who seek the true light. Dominates peace treaties, influences ambassadors.
Jerathel	131 to 135	Protects against unjust attacks, confounding one's enemies. Dominates civilisation and influences peace.
Seeiah	136 to 140	Protects agaist fire ruin and collapse. Dominates health and

longevity. Influences prudence.

Reiiel	141 to 145	Aids and protects against all enemies, both visible and invisible. Dominates mystical feelings and sacred philosophy.
Omael	146 to 150	Aids against desperation and trouble, also strengthens patience. Dominates the generation of men and animals.
Lecabel	151 to 155	Serves to cast light on one's job dominates vegetation. Influences astrology.
Vasariah	156 to 160	Aids against false, unjust accusations, dominates justice and judges. Influences the word.
Iehuiah	161 to 165	Serves to uncover plots and traitors in undoing their plans. Dominates and also influences just rulers.
Lehahiah	166 to 170	Helps maintain peace and harmony between countries. Dominates faithfulness respect and devotion.
Chevakiah	171 to 175	Helps recover the friendship of those we've offended. Dominates wills. Influences friendly distrubution.
Menadel	176 to 180	Conquer fears arising within you. Protects against slander

		and to release prisoners. Dominates the return of the exiled to their native land.
Aniel	181 to 185	Helps conquer and to obtain release from siege. Dominates the sciences and arts. Influences the meditation of the wise.
Haamiah	186 to 190	Protects against lightning and infernal spirits. Dominates creeds, influences and protects those who seek the truth.
Rehael	191 to 195	Protects and cures disease. Dominates health and longevity. Influences paternal love.
Ieiazel	196 to 200	Helps release prisoners and Frees us from enemies. Dominates the press and books. Influences artists.
Hahahel	201 to 205	Helps against the ungodly and slanderers. Dominates missionaries. Influences priests and prelates.
Mikael	206 to 210	Helps and protects the safety of journeys. Dominates the powerful. Influences curiosity and politics.
Veuahiah	211 to 215	Helps destroy enemies and freedom from slavery. Dominates peace. Influences

Prosperity.

Ielahiah	216 to 220	Protects and helps win a lawsuit. Dominates victory. Influences courage in battle.
Sealiah	221 to 225	Helps confound the evil and the proud. Dominates vegetation. Influences education.
Ariel	226 to 230	Helps rediscover hidden treasures. Dominates night-time visions. Influences difficult solutions.
Asaliah	231 to 235	Helps those who wish to raise themselves spiritually. Dominates justice. Influences contemplation.
Michael	236 to 240	Helps preserve harmony and union between spouses. Dominates the generations. Influences love.
Vehuel	241 to 245	Helps find peace against trouble. Dominates great personalities. Influences humility.
Daniel	246 to 250	Protects and consoles. Inspires in decision-making. Dominates justice and influences judges.
Hahasiah	251 to 255	Helps those who wish to know the occult mysteries. Dominates chemistry. Influences the abstract sciences.

Imamiah	256 to 260	Helps destroy enemies protects prisoners. Dominates vigor. Influences research.
Nanael	261 to 265	Serves to obtain enlightenment. Dominates the higher sciences. Influences teachers and men of law.
Nitael	266 to 270	Serves to obtain mercy and longevity. Dominates dynasties (kings,princes) and stability.
Mebaiah	271 to 275	Helps in consolation and those who wish to have children. Dominates morals, religion and piety.
Poiel	276 to 280	Serves to obtain what is asked for. Dominates fame, success and fortune. Influences moderation.
Nemamiah	281 to 285	Helps prosper and release prisoners. Dominates generals. Influences combatatants.
Leialel	286 to 290	Helps against trouble, heals eye diseases. Dominates iron. Influences locksmiths, knife-grinders etc.
Harakel	291 to 295	Protects against female sterility and rebellious children. Dominates treasures and archives. Influences the press.
Mizrael	296 to 300	Helps heal the ills of the spirit,

release from persecutors.
Dominates men of virtue.
Influences faithfulness.

Umabel	301 to 305	Serves to obtain the friendship of a person. Dominates astronomy and physics. Influences the sensitivity of the heart.
Iah-hel	306 to 310	Helps obtain wisdom and knowledge. Dominates philosophers and the enlightened. Influences virtue in solitude.
Anianuel	311 to 315	Protects against accidents, maintains health and heals. Dominates trade and businessmen. Influences business.
Mehiel	316 to 320	Protects against rabies and fierce animals. Dominates the learned, orators and authors. Influences the press, books etc.
Namabiah	321 to 325	Aids against sorcery and to obtain wisdom. Dominates the waters. Influences sailors, fisherman,etc.
Manakel	326 to 330	Protects against and heals leprosy. Also calms anger. Dominates vegetation. Influences sleep and dreams.

Etaiel	331 to 335	Helps and consoles in adversity and to obtain wisdom. Dominates change. Influences the occult sciences.
Xabuiah	336 to 340	Helps maintain health and cure disease. Dominates fertility, agriculture and the earth.
Rochel	341 to 345	Helps find lost or stolen objects dominates laws and judges. Influences fame.
Jabamiah	346 to 350	Protects and regenerates, leads to inner harmony. Dominates philosophical knowledge. Influences nature.
Haiel	351 to 355	Confounds the evil and grants release from enemies, gives victory. Dominates weapons and soldiers. Influences iron.
Mumiah	356 to 360	The last spirit. Brings every experience to a happy conclusion. Dominates medicine and influences longevity.

Angel Guardians of the Week

The angels who have authority over the seven days of the week-in much the same fashion as there are angels presiding over the planets, hours of the day, and months of the year. The angels give their particular day their special attention and in legend can be invoked to assist a person in some endeavor or need. The angels and their days are reported in The Magus (1801) by Francis Barrett:

Sunday-Michael
Monday-Gabriel
Tuesday-Camael
Wednesday-Raphael
Thursday-Sachiel
Friday-Anael
Saturday-Cassiel

Angel Guardians of the Month

January	Gabriel of Cambiel: Angel of Revelation and Chaos
February	Barchiel: Angel of Chance)
March	Machidiel (or Malhidael)
April	Asmodel
May:	Ambriel (or Almbriel)
June	Muriel
July	Verchiel
August	Hamaliel

September	Uriel (or Zuriel): Angel of Repentence
October	Barbiel
November	Adnachiel
December	Hanael or (Anael)

Angels of the Planets

Sun:	Michael
Moon:	Gabriel
Mercury:	Raphael
Venus:	Ariel
Mars:	Uriel
Jupiter:	Zadkiel or Zachariel
Saturn :	Orifiel or Zaphiel

Guardian Angels Categorized by the Metaphysical Elements and Months Corresponds to Physical Angel:

Guardian Angels of People Born under the Sign of Aries
Element: Fire

March 21 to 25:	VEHUIAH - One of eight Seraphim invoked to fulfill prayers. He governs the first rays of the sun.
March 26 to 30:	JELIEL - A Seraph whose name is inscribed on the Tree of Life. He is the Heavenly Prince Ruler of Turkey. He controls the destiny of kings and other high dignitaries and gives the palm of victory for those who are unjustly attacked or invaded. In addition he inspires passion between the sexes and insures marital fidelity.
March 31 to April 4:	SITAEL - A Seraph invoked to overcome adversity. He rules the nobility and is one of the 72 angels of the Zodiac; also one of the 72 angels that bear the name of God Shemhamphorae.
April 5 to 9:	ELEMIAH - One of the 8 Seraphim of the Tree of Life in the Book of Yesterday, and an angel (one of 72) bearing the mystical name of God Shemhamphorae. He rules over voyages and maritime expeditions. His corresponding angel is Senacher.
April 10 to 14:	MAHASIAH - One of 72 angels bearing the name of God Shemhamphorae
April 15 to 20:	LELAHEL - An angel of the zodiac exercising dominion over love, art, science and fortune. We appeal to this being of light for good luck and good fortune.

Guardian Angels of People born under the Sign of Taurus
Element: Earth

April 21 to 25:	ACHAIAH - He is a Seraphim, the angel of patience and discoverer of the secrets of nature. In the New Testament Achaiah is a Roman Province. Paul visited the churches in that region. (Acts 18:12, 27)
April 26 to 30:	CAHETEL - One of 8 Seraphim; he rules over agricultural products and is one of the 72 angels bearing the name of God Shemhamphorae. In the Cabala generally he is often invoked to increase or improve crops. His corresponding angel is Asicat.
May 1 to 5:	HAZIEL - A Cherub invoked to obtain the pity of God. He is one of 72 angels bearing the mystical name of God Shemhamphorae. When equated with Bernael, he is an angel of darkness. In 1st Chronicles 23:9 Haziel is mortal, an offspring of the Gershonites. The Cabalists very likely drew the name from this source.
May 6 to 10:	ALADIAH - One of the 72 angels bearing the name of God Shemhamphorae.
May 11 to 15:	LAUVIAH - In the Cabala, an angel of the order of Thrones; also of the order of Cherubim. More correctly, he formerly belonged to these orders. He influences savants and great personages.
May 16 to 20:	HAHAIAH - An angel of the order of Cherubim. He influences thoughts and reveals hidden mysteries to mortals.

Guardian Angels of People born under the Sign of Gemini
Element: Air

May 21 to 25:	IEZALEL - One of the angels of the Zodiac.
May 26 to 31:	MEBAHEL - One of the 72 angels bearing the name of God Shemhamphorae.
June 1 to 5:	HARIEL - Angel with dominion over tame beasts. He is invoked against impieties. He rules science and the arts and is of the order of Cherubim.
June 6 to 10:	HAKAMIAH - One of the Cherubim (invoked against traitors) and Guardian Angel of France. His corresponding angel is Verasua.
June 11 to 15:	LAUVIAH - In the Cabala, an angel of the order of Thrones; also of the order of Cherubim. More correctly, he formerly belonged to these orders. He influences savants and great personages.
June 16 to 21:	CALIEL - One of the Throne angels serving in the Second Heaven, invoked to bring prompt help during adversity. He is one of 72 angels bearing the mystical name of God Shemhamphorae. His corresponding angel is Tersatosoa (or Tepisatosa).

Guardian Angels of People born under the Sign of Cancer:
Element Water

June 22 to 26:	LEUUIAH - One of the 72 angels bearing the name of God Shemhamphorae.
June 27 to July 1:	PAHALIAH - An angel invoked to convert non-Christians to Christianity. He rules theology and morals and is one of the angels bearing the mystical name of the God Shemhamphorae. His corresponding angel is Sothis, who is an angel of an hour.
June 2 to July 6:	NELCHAEL - An angel belonging to the order of Thrones and one of the 72 angels bearing the name of God Shemhamphorae. However, he appears to be not a Holy Angel but a Fallen one who, in Hell, teaches astronomy, mathematics, and geography, to his fellow demons. His corresponding spirit is known as Sith.
July 7 to 11:	YEIAYEL - One of the angels of the Zodiac.
July 12 to 16:	MELAHEL - One of the 72 angels bearing the name of God Shemhamphorae.
July 17 to 22:	HAHUIAH - One of the 72 angels bearing the name of God Shemhamphorae.

Guardian Angels of People born under the Sign of Leo
Element: Fire

July 23 to 27:	NITHAIAH - A poet-angel of the order of Dominations. He is invoked by pronouncing any of the divine names along with the 1st verse of Psalm 9. He is in charge of occult sciences, delivers prophecies in rhyme, and exercises influence over wise men who love peace and solitude.
July 28 to August 1:	HAAIAH - An angel of the order of Dominations. He rules over diplomacy and ambassadors, and it one of the 72 angels bearing the name of God Shemhamphorae.
August 2 to 6:	YERATEL - An angel of the order of Dominations (Dominions). He "propagates light, civilization, and liberty." His corresponding angel is Hepe.
August 7 to 12:	SEHEIAH - An angel who provides protection against sickness and fire. He also governs longevity.
August 13 to 17:	REIIEL - An angel of the order of Dominations and is also one of the 72 angels bearing the name of God Shemhamphorae.
August 18 to 22:	OMAEL - An angel who multiplies species, perpetuates races and influences Chemists. There is some question as to whether Omael is a Fallen or Upright Angel. Data available suggests he seems to operate in both domains.

Guardian Angels of People born under the sign of Virgo
Element: Earth

August 23 to 28:	LECABEL - An angel in control of vegetation and agriculture, and one of the 72 angels bearing the mystical name of God Shemhamphorae.
August 29 to September 2:	VASAIRIAH - In the Cabala, an angel who rules over justice, nobility, magistrates, and lawyers.
September 3 to 7:	YEHUDIAH - In the Zohar, one of the chief angelic envoys. He descends with myriads of attending angels for the purpose of bearing aloft the souls of the persons about to die, or who have just died. He is a beneficent Angel of Death.
September 8 to 12:	LEHAHIAH - Once of the order of Powers (Potentates), he protects crowned heads and makes subjects obedient to their superiors. He is (or was, depending on his current status as a holy or evil angel) one of the 72 heirarchs bearing the mystical name of God Shemhamphorae.
September 13 to 17:	CHAVAKIAH - One of the 72 angels bearing the name of God Shemhamphorae.
September 18 to 23:	MENADEL - An angel of the order of Powers; also one of the 72 angels of the Zodiac. Menadel keeps exiles faithful or loyal to their native land. His corresponding angel, in the Cabala, is Aphut.

Guardian Angel of People born under the Sign of Libra
Element: Air

September 24 to 28:	ANIEL - One of the numerous angelic guards of the gates of the West wind.
September 29 to October 3:	HAAMIAH - An angel of the order of Powers. He dominates religious cults and "protects all those who seek the truth." His corresponding angel (in the Cabala) is Serucuth.
October 4 to 8:	REHAEL - An angel of the order of Powers. He rules over health and longevity, and inspires respect for one's parents. He is one of the 72 angels bearing the mystical name of God Shemhamphorae. His corresponding angel is Ptechout.
October 9 to 13:	IHIAZEL - One of the 72 angels bearing the name of God Shemhamphorae.
October 14 to 18:	HAHAHEL - Hahahel is also spelled Hahael and this angel in an angel of the order of Virtues. Hahael protects missionaries and all disciples. He is also one of the 72 angels bearing the mystical name of the God Shemhamphorae. His corresponding angel is Chantare`, who's description only states that he is the corresponding angel to Hahahel (Hahael).
October 19 to 23:	MIKAEL - An angel who influences the decisions of monarchs, nobles, and governors; also useful in uncovering conspiracies against states. His corresponding angel is Arpien.

Guardian Angels of People born under the Sign of Scorpio
Element: Water

October 24 to 28:	VEULIAH - An angel of the order of Principalities; also a Zodiac angel and he is also one of the 72 angels bearing the mystical name of the God Shemhamphorae.
October 29 to November 2:	YELAIAH - One of the angels of the Zodiac.
November 3 to 7:	SAELIAH - In the Cabala, a Fallen angel once of the order of Virtues. He has (or had) dominion over vegetables. When invoking him, and for the best results, it is advisable to recite a verse from Psalm 93.
November 8 to 12:	ARIEL - Ranks as one of the 7 Princes who rule the waters and is "Earth's Great Lord." In occult writings, he is the "3rd archon of the winds." He is also the angel who assists Raphael in the cure of disease. He is in charge of punishment in the Lower World, controls demons, and is ruler of winds. In practical Cabala he is regarded as originally of the order of Virtues. He is known to be a conglomerate of Anael and Uriel, a Sprite, and a Rebel Angel, according to different sources.
November 13 to 17:	ASALIAH - In the Cabala, an angel of the order of Virtues, under the ethnarchy of Raphael. He has dominion over justice. One of the 72 angels bearing the mystical name of God Shemhamphorae.
November 18 to 22:	MIHAEL - In the Cabala, an angel in control of conjugal fidelity and fertility. He belongs to the order of Virtues and is one of the 72 angels bearing the name of God Shemhamphorae.

Guardian Angel of People born under the Sign of Sagittarius
Element: Fire

November 23 to 27:	VEHUEL - An angel of the order of Principalities; also a Zodiac angel and one of the 72 angels bearing the name of God Shemhamphorae.
November 28 to December 2:	DANIEL - An angel of the order of Principalities. He exercises dominion over lawyers. He is a high Holy Angel who bears the name of Shemhamphorae.
December 3 to 7:	HAHAZIAH - One of the 72 angels bearing the name of God Shemhamphorae.
December 8 to 12:	IMAMIAH - In the Cabala, an angel of the order of Principalities, or rather and ex-angel of that order, since he is fallen. In Hell he supervises and controls voyages,and destroys and humiliates enemies, when he is invoked to do so, or is so disposed. He was once one of the 72 angels that bore the name of God Shemhamphorae.
December 13 to 16:	NANAEL - In practical Cabala, one of the Principalities; also one of the 72 angels bearing the mystical name of God Shemhamphorae. Exercises dominion over the great sciences, influences philosophers and ecclesiastics. His corresponding angel is Chomme.
December 17 to 21:	NITHAEL - In the Cabala, an angel formerly of the order of Principalities. One of the 72 angels bearing the name of God Shemhamphorae. The prevailing belief is that Nithael joined Satan during the rebellion in Heaven and that now, in Hell, he governs emperors and kings, also civil and ecclesiastical personages of the highest rank.

Guardian Angels of People Born under the Sign of Capricorn
Element: Earth

December 22 to 26:	MEBAHIAH - An angel who exercises dominion over morality and religion. He also helps those desiring offspring.
December 27 to 31:	POIEL - An angel of the order of Principalities. He rules over fortune and philosophy. He also is one of the 72 angels of the Zodiac.
January 1 to 5:	NEMAMIAH - This sacred being is a guardian angel of all those who fight for just causes. He is especially protective towards people who defend the rights of those who cannot defend themselves, such as animals and children. When an injustice is done towards anyone, including ourselves, we can pray to Nemamiah to right the wrong.
January 6 to 10:	IEILAEL - One of the 72 angels bearing the name of God Shemhamphorae.
January 11 to 15:	HARAEL - This radiant one protects libraries, archives, schools and universities. Harahel opens our minds and hearts to new ideas while inspiring humankind to use this knowledge in life-affirming ways.
January 16 to 20:	MITZRAEL - One of the archangels in Cabalistic lore. Induces obedience on the part of inferiors toward superiors. One of the 72 angels bearing the name of God Shemhamphorae. His corresponding angel is Homoth.

Guardian Angels of People born under the Sign of Aquarius
Element: Air

January 21 to 25:	UMABEL - In the Cabala, Umabel is said to have dominion over physics and astronomy. He is also one of the 72 angels bearing the mystical name of God Shemhamphorae. His corresponding angel is Ptiau.
January 26 to 30:	IAHHEL - This shining one inspires meditation and illumination. Iahhel watches over philosophers and those who seek a retreat from worldly pursuits. For those who have difficulty meditating, pray to Iahhel for help just before you begin your meditative practice.
January 31 to February 4:	ANAUEL - An angel who protects commerce, bankers, commission brokers, etc. His corresponding angel is Aseij.
February 5 to 9:	MEHIEL - An angel who protects university professors, orators and authors.
February 10 to 14:	DAMABIAH - An angel of the order of angels with dominion over naval construction.
February 15 to 19:	MANAKEL - Angel of aquatic animals.

Guardian Angel of People born under the Sign of Pisces
Element: Water

February 20 to 24:	EIAEL - An angel with dominion over occult sciences, longevity, etc. One of the 72 angels bearing the mystical name of God Shemhamphorae. His corresponding angel is Abiou. When Eiael is conjured up, the invocate must recite the 4th verse of Psalm 36.
February 25 to 28:	HABUIAH - An angel who exercises dominion over agriculture and fecundity. One of the 72 angels bearing the name of God Shemhamphorae.
March 1 to 5:	ROCHEL - An angel who finds lost objects.
March 6 to 10:	GABAMIAH - In Solomonic Goetic rites, a great angel invoked by the use of incantatory power of the name of the angel Uriel.
March 11 to 15:	HAIAIEL - One of the 72 angels of the Zodiac and one of the 72 angels bearing the name of God Shemhamphorae.
March 16 to 20:	MUMIAH - This angel presides over the sciences of medicine and physics. Mumiah is traditionally believed to grant health and longevity, as well as being able to suspend physical laws to create miracles.

Afterword:

The angels each have a spiritual, physical and emotional aspect which makes a total of three angels assigned to each and every person on the day and time and year of their birth. Please visit my website to get a full angel reading.

Keep in mind an angel may be called upon to assist through God for a particular issue you may have, however it is important to know and recognize your specific angels in their guardian manifest in your life.

By invoking Angels as a manifestation of God you transmit various blends of energy into your physical world. The very rich tradition of the Angelology can thus accompany modern man in the tests of life and lead us on a way of progression to all material, mental and spiritual levels.

What are the roles of these nine hierarchies?

THE SACRED CALENDAR

Important Month numbers to know. Note: that most of the Bible refers to months by number, not by name

The Sacred Calendar:

English Equivalent of Month	Number	Length	Hebraic Name
March-April	1	30 days	Nissan
April-May	2	29days	Iyar
May-June	3	30days	Sivan
June-July	4	29 days	Tammuz
July-August	5	30 days	Av
August-September	6	29 days	Elul
September-October	7	30 days	Tishri
October-November	8	29 -30 days	Cheshvan
November-December	9	30-29 days	Kislev
December-January	10	29 days	Tevet
January-February	11	30 days	Shevat
February-March	12	30 days	Adar I
February-March	12/13	29 days In leap year	Adar II (in leap years)

Patron Angels: (Work with the 72 Guardian Angels

Adversity - Mastema
Agriculture - Rismuch
Air - Chasam
Alchemy - Och
Anger - Af
Annihilation - Harbonah
Apocalypse - Orifiel
Birds - Arael
Chance - Barakiel
Chaos - Michael or Satan
Comets - Aiqiel
Compassion - Raphael
Conception - Lailah
Dawn - Lucifer
Day - Shamshiel
Destiny – Oriel
Doom – Dooma *grinds a body to dust in the grave, because of severe transgressions
Dreams - Duma
Dust - Saphlatus
Earthquakes - Rashiel
Embryo - Sandalphon

Fear - Yroul
Fertility - Samandiriel
Fire - Nathanael
Forests - Azphlas
Free Will - Tabris
Friendship - Mihr
Glory - Sandalphon
Grace - Ananchel
Hail - Bardiel
Healing - Raphael
Health - Mumiel
Hope - Phanuel
Hurricanes - Zaapiel
Insomnia - Michael
Justice - Tzadkiel
Knowledge - Raphael
Light - Isaac
Lightning - Baraqiel
Love - Theliel
Memory - Zadkiel
Mountals - Rampel
Music - Israfel
Night - Leliel
Obedience - Sraosha
Oblivion - Purah

Order - Sadriel
Patience - Achaiah
Penance - Phamuel
Poetry - Israfel
Pride - Rahab
Progress - Raphael
Prostitution - Eisheth
Purity - Tahariel
Rain - Macariel
Repentance - Uriel
Revelation - Gabriel
Righteousness - Michael
Sea - Rahab
Silence - Shatetiel
Snow - Salgiel
Stars - Kokabiel
Strength - Zeruel
Thunder - Ra'amiel
Treasures - Parasiel
Truth - Amitiel
Twilight - Aftiel
War - Michael
Weakness - Amaliel
Whirlwind - Zaamiel
Wind - Ruhiel

Womb - Armisael

BIBLIOGRAPHY

The Holy Bible
Berg, Yehuda, *The 72 Names of God – Technology for the Soul*
Bunson, Matthew, *Angels A to Z*
Briggs, Victoria Constanc, *The Encyclopedia of Angels*
Cyberre.com
Daniel D. Kudra
Esotericharchives.com
Leah, Sarah www.hebrewletters.com
Higgins, Godfrey, *Anacalypsis, An Inquiry into the Origin of Languages, Nations and Religions*
Mazzaroth.com
Vallowe, Ed
Virtue, Doreen

Source: 2letterlookupdotcom

Addendum

Miracle HafTorah

Parshas Beshalach
Shoftim 4:4

by Rabbi Dovid Siegel

This week's haftorah shows the effect of the Jewish nation's faith in Hashem irrespective of their level of mitzva observance. After the passing of Moshe Rabbeinu's devout disciple, Joshua the Jewish people were led by numerous judges. Their authority and influence was considerably limited and the Jewish people adopted foreign cultures and strayed from the Torah's ways. They typically fluctuated between sincere service of Hashem and repulsive idolatry. Hashem would respond to their abhorrent behavior and release one of the powerful nations to oppress them. The Jewish people would hear the message and sincerely return to Hashem until they succumbed again to foreign influences.

This week's haftorah speaks of one of those times when the Jewish nation severely strayed from the path. Hashem responded and permitted Yovin, the king of Canaan to capture the Jewish nation and annex her to his mighty empire. After twenty years of firm control the message hit home and the Jewish people began to repent. Hashem recognized their initial stages of repentance and sent the Prophetess Devorah to help them complete the process. They merited through her efforts an incredible miracle and Devorah composed a moving song of praise describing Hashem's revelations.

The miracle occurred when Devora instructed the leading Jewish general, Barak to select ten thousand men and charge into the Canaanite lines. Yovin gathered an army of hundreds of thousands and planned a massive attack against the Jewish people. Hashem intervened on behalf of His people and created an illusion of enormous proportions forcing the Canaanites to flee for their lives. In the midst of this, Hashem sent blazing heat to the battle front and brought the Canaanites down to the Kishon Brook to cool off. At that exact moment, Hashem caused the brook to overflow and drown the Canaanites. Devorah sang about this miracle and said, "Kishon Brook swept them away - that brook of age my soul treads with strength." (Shoftim 5: 21) Devorah referred to the Kishon as a brook of age seeming to relate it an earlier experience.

Chazal explain that this earlier incident was, in fact, the splitting of the Sea of Reeds recorded in this week's parsha. They quote an intriguing conversation between Hashem and the angel appointed over the sea of Reeds. Chazal reflect upon a verse in Tehillim (106:7) that indicates the Jewish people's imperfect faith while crossing the sea. Chazal explain that although the entire nation heard Moshe Rabbeinu's prediction of Egypt's downfall at the sea many found it difficult to accept in full. Hence, after the sea miraculously opened they entertained the possibility that Egyptians were also safely crossing and would continue their chase. *The Jewish people felt undeserving of a miracle performed solely for their sake and reasoned that the sea split in numerous places. Hashem dispelled this fiction and instructed the angel over the Sea of Reeds to cast the dying Egyptians onto shore. When the Jewish people saw this they understood retroactively what truly transpired for them. Note from Author: this explains possibly why VHV appears twice as 1st Name of G-d and 49th Name of G-d. VHV called the East Wind to separate the Sea, Announcement by G-d of Rescue and the instruction for Moses to stretch out right hand to begin the process of the Miracle Passage.* The angel, however, argued that the fish deserved their promised prize of thousands of Egyptian bodies and requested a replacement in the future. Hashem consented and informed the angel that the Kishon Brook would eventually sweep replacements into the sea and grant the fish their earlier present. (Mesichta Pesachim 115b)

The above discussion suggests a direct corollary between the splitting of the Sea of Reeds and the overflowing Kishon Brook. It points to a missing dimension of faith at the sea that was ultimately rectified through the Kishon Brook. The analogy of the fish reflects the Jewish people's imperfect perception of Hashem's miracles. The splitting of the sea served a dual function- to rescue the Jewish people and to punish the Egyptian nation. The first function was fully accomplished however the second was not. Although the mighty Yam Suf waters delivered the Egyptians their fair share of brutal torture it did not drown them. In essence, the sea played an imperfect role in Hashem's miraculous scheme. This undoubtedly reflected the Jewish people's imperfect faith in Hashem's miracles and concern for His people. The angel of the sea responded to Hashem that the sea deserved a perfect role in Hashem's miracles and should be granted future opportunity for a perfect revelation of Hashem's might. Hashem responded to the angel that the miracle of the Kishon Brook would serve this capacity in full.

In the days of the prophetess Devorah the Jewish people's spiritual level suffered serious decline. They shared similar feelings with the Jewish people at the Sea of Reeds and feel unworthy of great revelations. They recently began their long process of return and could not imagine Hashem performing miracles on their behalf. However, when Devora instructed Barak to select ten 8nthousand men and charge into the massive Canaanite army he immediately accepted his role. He and his men demonstrated total faith in Hashem and believed wholeheartedly that Hashem would perform an open miracle solely on their behalf. Although their level of spirituality was far from perfect they displayed total faith in Hashem. This time they had no doubts and Hashem did not need to prove His involvement on behalf of His people. The sea was therefore granted its full role and its fish eagerly devoured the wicked Canaanites sent to it by the Kishon brook. This miracle was unequivocally clear and bore testimony to all of Hashem's absolute commitment to His people and total involvement on their behalf. Although their mitzva observance was far from perfect they were sincerely committed to rectifying it and deserved Hashem's grace and favor.

We learn from this the power of absolute trust in Hashem. Many question how the present Jewish people could deserve to witness the miraculous era of Mashiach. Our spiritual level is far from perfect and certainly does not warrant Hashem's intervention on our behalf. Let us draw strength and encouragement from our Haftorah's lesson and realize what Hashem expects from us. The road to return is undoubtedly long, however, Hashem only asks for sincerity. Let us resolve to follow Hashem's lead wherever He takes us and trust that He cares for us in untold proportions. In this merit we will hopefully be privileged to witness Hashem's greatest revelations ever to be seen, surpassing even those in Egypt and at the Sea of Reeds.

Source: Torahdotorg

Another Analysis of Miracle Passage HafToroh

Judges 4:4-5:31.

This week's haftorah describes the fall of the Canaanite general Sisera and his armies, who were swept away by the Kishon River, and Deborah's ensuing song of thanks. This parallels this week's Torah portion which discusses the drowning of the Egyptian forces in the Red Sea and and the subsequent songs led by Moses and Miriam.

Deborah the Prophetess was the leader and judge of the Israelites at a difficult time; the Israelites were being persecuted by King Jabin of Canaan and his general Sisera. Deborah summoned Barak son of Abinoam and transmitted to him G-d's instruction: "Go and gather your men toward Mount Tabor, and take with you ten thousand men of the children of Naphtali and Zebulun. And I shall draw to you, to the brook Kishon, Sisera, the chieftain of Jabin's army, with his chariots and his multitude; and I will give him into your hand." At Barak's request, Deborah accompanied him, and together they led the offensive.

Sisera was informed of the Israelites' mobilization and he gathered his forces and proceeded towards the Kishon River. Barak's army below and the heavens above waged battle against the Canaanites and utterly destroyed them. The river washed them all away; not one of the enemy survived.

The defeated general fled on foot and arrived at the tent of Jael, wife of Heber the Kenite. She invited him in and offered to hide him. When he fell asleep, Jael took a tent-peg and knocked it through Sisera's temple.

The next chapter of the haftorah is the Song of Deborah, which describes the miraculous victory and thanks the One Above for His assistance.
Source: Chabaddotorg

Moses conversation with G-d when the Angels protested his presence in the upper world

Do not murder. Do not commit adultery. Do not steal (20:13)

When Moses ascended to heaven, the angels protested to G-d: "What is a human being doing amongst us?"

Said He to them: "He has come to receive the Torah."

Said they to Him: "This esoteric treasure, which was hidden with You for nine hundred and seventy-four generations before the world was created, You wish